SUICIDE

SOME REFLECTIONS

Our time is fixed, and all our days are numbered,
How long, how short, we know not—this we know
Duty requires we calmly wait the summons,
Not dare to stir till Heaven shall give permission

Robert Blair, The Grave, 1.417

SUICIDE
SOME REFLECTIONS

Editor
Kusum

Foreword
Justice (Retd.) Rajindar Sachar

Regency Publications
New Delhi-110 008

ISBN 81-86030-08-5

Published by Regency Publications, 20/36-G, Old Market, West Patel Nagar, New Delhi-110008 and Printed at Radiant Printers, New Delhi-110008, Phones: 5713968, 5783571

FOREWORD

I have great pleasure in writing a foreword to the book *Suicide: Some Reflections*, edited by Kusum of the Indian Law Institute, New Delhi. She has, in addition to her own contribution, consolidated views of a number of eminent experts on different aspects of the problem of suicide and displayed her ability and scholarly aptitude in bringing them together.

This book contains thirteen chapters—each delineating a particular aspect of the problem of suicide. The first chapter deals with the important question as to whether man has the inherent right to end his life. In fact, this question has kicked up considerable dust in the wake of the Supreme Court judgement and through an interesting discussion on the verdict of the apex court the author has brought into focus the wider implications of this judgement on the existing social milieu. Similarly, the second chapter gives a brilliant analysis of the positive aspect of the fundamental right to life as enshrined in Article 21 of the Constitution with particular reference to the judgement of the Supreme Court.

The third chapter highlights an interesting topic on the relationship between suicide and life insurance. The author has presented his views in a lucid manner giving an explicit idea about the historical background and the content of life insurance policy. He has discussed in detail the positions in respect of this problem in other developed countries like England and America citing a large number of decisions by the courts.

In the following chapters, viz., four, five, six, seven, eight and nine, the authors have dwelt at length on the pros and cons of the problem of suicide against the background of the latest judgement of the apex court holding Section 309 I.P.C. as unconstitutional. A plethora of ideas emerge out of these discussions and give rise to the scope for wide spread debates and conclaves.

The tenth chapter makes a study of the problem from a different angle and brings into focus its psychosocial aspects. The author has extensively surveyed the conditions in respect of suicide in various countries and mentioned the age-old traditional social norms inhibiting suicide in India. A discussion on various methods of suicide prevailing in different societies together with some important physical and psychological causes makes this chapter all the more interesting. The social responsibility of the members of the community in tackling this problem and how they can be involved actively in the planning, organisation and maintenance of an all-embracing programme for this purpose have been emphasised. The author's suggestion of a multi-disciplinary approach including psychology, psychiatry, social work, theology, sociology, philosophy, forensic science, etc., is very practical and worthy to be taken into consideration while thinking in terms of any suicide-prevention programme.

The eleventh chapter is replete with a number of stories depicting the compelling circumstances under which an individual commits suicide or seeks to exterminate the entire family along with himself. The author has comprehensively dealt with the problem of suicide from different angles.

While dwelling on the different aspects of the problem of suicide, the author has rightly devoted a major part of his discussion on the preventive measures in the twelfth chapter. His suggestion for introducing some methods for detecting the vulnerable cases and taking timely action are immensely useful and merit consideration by appropriate authorities.

In the last chapter the author has dealt with the pros and cons of this problem very exhaustively and presented a balanced view with an eye to the future implications of the latest judgement of Supreme Court.

Frankly speaking I had always maintained and that was the view I took in one of my judgement in 1985 that this provision was an anachronism unworthy of any civilised society.

Some apprehend that as suicide is no longer punishable, it will lead to increase in such cases. To me such fear is laughable. A person who is willing to end his/her life is not deterred by the fear of Court's punishment. He/she has gone beyond these petty calculations. Deterrence may have some effect on crime—but it is obnoxious to think that a person committing suicide is a criminal. If anybody has to be held responsible, it is not that unfortunate individual, but the society, which has created ugly situations. What was more painful to me was to find that the majority of persons who were being prosecuted under Section 309 I.P.C were the poorer sections of the society. Is that, I ask, why this provision continued on the statute book notwithstanding even the recommendations of the Law Commission as far back as 1971 to delete it? This judgement of the Supreme Court again shows how the courts are in the vanguard of radicalisation of social and political thinking; against the status quoist attitude of politicians always overlooking their shoulders for electoral advantages.

In the recent past books on suicide have appeared and among them this book, which is definitely a welcome addition to the literature on suicide, will occupy a high position. The significance of this book is that it will meet the critical need for a text which will serve as an essential source for anyone interested in acquiring thoughtful and provocative viewpoints about various issues on suicide. It will prove of great value to those in the fields of law, social work, social sciences and other related disciplines. I do hope that this book will inspire contemplation in readers and provoke further debates and discussions on the subject.

February 4, 1995

Justice (Retd.) Rajindar Sachar
Former Chief Justice of
Delhi High Court

EDITOR'S NOTE

It is pertinent to note that just four months after *Nagabhushan* declaring Section 309, I.P.C. as *ultra vires*, the Supreme Court itself has upheld a conviction for attempted suicide in *Vijay alias Gian Chand Jain* v. *State of M.P.* (JT 1994(5) S.528 decided on September 2, 1994). The sessions judge convicted and sentenced the accused for murder of his wife and later attempting to commit suicide. The High Court upheld this conviction. The appellant's further appeal to the Supreme Court was dismissed. The Court discussed the issue of tenability of conviction for murder without even explicitly referring to Section 309. It simply stated, "we find no reason to interfere with the order of conviction and sentence passed against the appellant" which included upholding conviction for attempted suicide. One wonders what would be the impact of this judgement on the issue of attempted suicide because it has come after *Nagabhushan* and this also was decided by a bench of two. In order to avoid vagueness and confusion it is essential that a clarification be made on the point expeditiously either by a larger bench *suo moto* or by legislative amendment.

PREFACE

The right to take one's own life has been a much debated subject all over the world. Many countries have long back statutorily recognised the right of a person to commit suicide. The debate has been on in our country too but the act of attempted suicide continues to be an offence under our Penal Code. Thus, a person who succeeds in taking away his life escapes all worldly miseries as well as legal action whereas one whose attempt fails is drawn into the dragnet of criminal courts. The Supreme Court judgement in *Nagabhushan* (1994) declaring Section 309 of the Penal Code, which penalises attempted suicide, as *ultra vires* the Constitution has evoked a mixed response.

This small book is a collection of articles on the subject by scholars from various disciplines. Diverse issues connected with the act of attempted suicide have been discussed and analysed.

I am extremely grateful to all the learned authors who acceded to my request and have given their valuable contributions. I must also thank the printers for the meticulous handling of the book and the artist for the excellent jacket design.

Kusum

When all the blandishments of life, are gone,
The coward sneaks to death
The brave live on

Martial, Epigrams BKxi, 56

CONTENTS

This life is a fort committed to my trust,
which I must not yield uptil it be forced,
Nor will I. He's not valiant that dares die,
But he that boldly bears calamity

Massinger, The Maid of Honour Act IV, SC 3

Chapter 1

THE RIGHT TO DIE

S. Sahay*

AS WAS only to be expected, the Supreme Court judgement[1] declaring Section 309 of the Indian Penal Code, which declares attempted suicide to be an offence, as unconstitutional, has attempted faint prise even from the legal experts. Senior advocate P.P. Rao has wondered whether this "investigative judicial review" was the only way of mitigating the harshness of the Indian Penal Code provision and whether a larger bench should not have decided the issue. Ashok Desai, another Senior advocate has talked about the grey areas of abetment to suicide. Soli Sorabjee has said that the court should have taken the help of other agencies, including pyschologists, psychiatrists and considered the wider dimensions of the problem. P.M. Bakshi, member Law Commission feels that the court has brought down suicide from the highest pedestal of punishability but there is still the question of where the court has left it.

This writer is of the considered view that by going far beyond the legal and constitutional questions and trying to delve into the mysteries of life and death, the court has opened a Pandora's box. A woman may be brought up into believing that life bereft of a husband is both wrong and meaningless, virtue in the next life is what matters and hence the best way to earn it is to perish on the husband's funeral pyre. A bride being tortured for dowry may think that death would be an

* Journalist, Former Editor *Statesman* and a Columnist.

escape. In the light of the Supreme Court judgement all that the hapless widow or the bride needs to do is to leave a statement saying that she is voluntarily committing Sati or taking away her life, that nobody is responsible for her action and that would be the end of the matter. Proving abetment in such case is already difficult and would be more so in future.

Thus the Supreme Court judgement has graver implications than mere non-punishment for an attempt to commit suicide and the problem has been created by the court's own decision to be comprehensive rather than precise. It asked no less than 15 questions: among these were whether suicide was a non-religious act, also, whether suicide was immoral.

As for the first question, it referred to an article by G.P. Tripathi in which the author had referred to the Hindu view that everyman lived to accomplish four objectives: *Dharma*, *Artha*, *Kama* and *Moksha*. Once these earthly objectives were achieved, religion would not require a person to cling to his body, for, death merely implied changing the old body for a new one.

The Court also referred to the encyclopaedia of religion and quoted its view on life. The book says that the very act of posing the question what is life, produces an initial sense of bafflement and perplexity, that the very question brings into belief the fact that life is an inexhaustible store house of mysteries, a realm of endlessly perpetuating novelties, in which the solution to given problem give rise to a plethora of other questions that beacon the always restless, never contented mind of the homosapiens to search out more intellectually refined, morally elevating and spiritually salutary ways of pursuing the quest.

The Court went on to conclude that life did not end in this world and the quest continued, may be after the end of this life. Therefore, one who took his life may not really have put an end to his whole life. There was thus nothing against religion in what he did.

The Court then referred to our mythology and talked of Lord Rama and his brothers taking *jalasamadhi* and of fasts by Mahatma Gandhi and Vinoba Bhave, which results in the latter's death. It concluded by observing that any allegation that these great personages indulged in non-religious acts would be considered a sacrilege. So where was non-religiosity in the act of suicide, it asked.

One is not sure whether it was at all necessary for the court to consider whether suicide was a non-religious act. One's diffidence is based on the fact that our laws are based on the premise that, at the State level, the present life is all that matters and that it governs both believers and non-believers. By considering questions of life after death the court seems to have travelled beyond its jurisdiction. It's quoting of mythology which talks of *jalasamadhi* by Lord Rama and his brothers and the courting of death by Buddha and Mahavira and the various fasts by Mahatma Gandhi and Vinoba Bhave is likely to send the wrong signals to ordinary people. How can you ever prevent voluntary sati after this judgement? What the court has forgotten is that the conduct and value judgements of our saints and *rishis*—highly evolved persons—cannot determine the conduct of an average person. Theoretically it should be possible to brainwash the Hindu women into believing that sati is the best passport to future bliss. And what would the State do if a woman were to declare before any authority that she voluntarily wanted to perish with her husband?

Happily, it would not be possible for the State to propagate suicide as a solution to the population problem, because the court has made a distinction between a voluntary decision and one induced by the State or any other organisation. It has also not dealt with euthanasia although it seems to be in sympathy.

As for the question whether suicide was immoral, the Court concluded that morality had no defined contours, that it would be too hazardous to make the bold statement, that the commission of suicide per se was immoral. "If human beings can be treated inhumanly, as a very large segment of our population is, which in significant measure is due to wrong (immoral) act of others, charge of immorality cannot be, and should not be, levied if such human beings or likes of them feel and think that it would be better to end the wretched life instead of allowing further humiliation or torture."

Strictly from the legal and constitutional point of view, the judgement is more a culmination of recent thinking on the issue in the country than a pace-setting ruling.

This is clear from the judgement delivered by Justice Hansaria, the other judge on the bench being Justice R.M. Sahai. The judge has recalled three High Court judgments on the issue and taken note of the Law Commission's recommendations, the steps taken by Parliament to implement them and the views of various experts expressed from time to time. This is as it should be for, in the ultimate analysis the foundation of law is ethics, the felt needs and perceptions of a particular society at a particular time.

As far as the judiciary is concerned, it was Justice Rajinder Sachar who as early as 1985,[2] found it strange that, in the age of euthanasia suicide should be criminally punishable, that the society which drives a young man to despair and suicide rather than hang its head in shame, treats him as criminal. He stressed the need for a humane, civilised, and socially oriented outlook and penology. He had been called upon to decide the question of whether investigation of a case involving attempted suicide should be allowed to continue beyond the period contemplated by the Criminal Procedure Code.

Two years later, the constitutionality of Section 309 was challenged before the Bombay High Court.[3] Justice Sawant declared it violative of Article 14 (the right to equality) and Article 21 (the right to life) of the Constitution.

Later the same question arose before the Andhra Pradesh High Court too.[4] It held the section to be valid.

The Delhi High Court suo motu considered the question once again but rather than strike down Section 309 it quashed all the 119 proceedings pending in the trial courts.

These decisions were commented upon by experts, including the former late Chief Justice of the Delhi High Court, late Justice V.S. Despande. (The title of the present article has been borrowed from the title Justice Despande gave to his own article.)

The Law Commission's thinking preceded judicial consideration on the subject. As early as 1971, it declared punishment of attempted suicide as harsh and unjustifiable. The Government accepted its recommendation and a Bill was introduced in the Rajya Sabha to repeal the section. It was referred to a Joint Select Committee. After receiving its report, the Rajya Sabha adopted the Bill with some changes but the Lok Sabha was dissolved in 1979 before it could pass the Bill. However the present Government has admitted to the court that it too considers Section 309 to be harsh.

Hence the point to note is that what the Division Bench of the Supreme Court has done is nothing radical or out of tune with the country's thinking on the subject. It has done what Parliament failed to do because the Lok Sabha was dissolved and the Bill lapsed.

The constitutional question before the Supreme Court[5] was whether Section 309 of the Penal Code offends Article 14 and 21. The Division Bench agreed with the views of the Bombay High Court concerning Article 21 but agreed with the Andhra High Court on Article 14. It said that the Bombay High Court had declared Section 309 to be violative of Article 14 mainly on two grounds. The first ground was that it was difficult to draw the line on what ultimately constituted suicide, that even philosophers, moralists and sociologists were not agreed on what constituted suicide. In the absence of guidelines, Section 309 was arbitrary. The second reason given by the Bombay High Court was that all suicides were treated by the same yardstick, the circumstances in which these were made were not at all taken into account.

Justice Hansaria of the Supreme Court felt that the first reason given by the Bombay High Court was not convincing because irrespective of what constituted suicide there was no doubt that it consisted in intentionally taking away one's life. Anyway, it was always open to the accused to plead that his attempt did not amount to attempted suicide and the court would have to consider it. The second reason was faulty because punishment could always be tailored to meet the gravity of the crime.

All one can say is that the Supreme Court's rather summary rejection of Section 309 offending Article 14 is not persuasive enough but since the court has concentrated mainly on Section 309 offending Article 21, let us concentrate on that. The question it has asked is whether Article 21 has any positive content or is it merely negative in its reach. This question, according to the court has been answered time and again and especially in the 'right to education' case. In that case the judges have listed, on the basis of earlier decisions, the right to life, including the right to privacy, the right against solitary confinement and against handcuffing, to name only a few, as inherent in the right to life, and have themselves added the right to primary education. These are enough to indicate that the right to life has a positive content, that it means more than mere animal existence.

The next legal question asked is whether a person living in this country has the right to die. Justice Hansaria agrees with the Bombay High Court that just as the freedom of speech includes the freedom of silence or the freedom to indulge in trade includes the freedom not to do so, likewise the freedom to live should imply the freedom not to live. It agrees with the critics of that view only to the extent that the negative aspect may not necessarily be inferable from the positive aspects of Article 19.

What is important is that the Supreme Court Division Bench has held that a person cannot be forced to enjoy the right to life to his detriment, disadvantage or dislike. In its view one may rightly think that having attained all worldly pleasures or happiness one had better do something to achieve in the life beyond. Thus the right to live does include the right not to lead a forced life.

There is a discussion in the judgement as to why a particular law is enacted and what purpose it serves. Macaulay, who drafted the Indian Penal Code, believed in the efficacy of the law in improving the people and their character. The noble Lord thought that a good system of law and police would improve the national character. Of course, his views are now disowned even in his home land and the fact of the matter is that even sodomy, of which Macaulay took such a stern view, has not only been legalised but the age of consent has been lowered.

Law is the proverbial laggard. It has to keep up with the times but in doing so it has to take into account not only the ethos and the philosophy of the country but also the progress in knowledge and the experience of other countries to the extent they are applicable to this country. The court has, as already indicated, thought the same way as the country does but it has taken on more than it could have competently tackled. It has acted where Parliament failed. May be it is the turn of Parliament to take off from where the court has left and have a really comprehensive legislation on the subject.

The court has dealt with the question as to why suicide is committed. Its analysis is bookish, as it is bound to be in the absence of expertise in the field. It has referred to the Bible, the Quran and the Rig Veda. It has referred to Greek fables. It has said that the causes of suicide are many. It could be caused by exasperation, fury, frustration and revolution. It could result from a feeling of burden, torture and sadness. It could be caused by loss of employment, reversal of fortune, family trouble and thwarted love. It could be caused by a feeling of unjust treatment. This is good as far as it goes but the Indian society needs to think deeply whether suicides could be prevented and what it could do about it.

According to a report published in the Indian Express the latest figures available with the National Criminal Records Bureau show that the number of suicides has jumped from 48,245 in 1981 to 80,149 in 1992. The reason for this is rapid industrialisation which has disoriented people's way of life and which has had a definite role to play in the increase in the number of suicides. The court has held that attempted suicide is a call for help and not a crime. Timely counselling is important. How this can be done on a large-scale is the question.

END NOTES

1. *P. Rathinam/Nagabhushan Patnaik* v. *Union of India.* J.T. 1994 (3) SC 392.
2. *State* v. *Sanjay Kumar.* 1985 Cri. L.J. 931 (Delhi).
3. *Maruti Shripati* v. *State of Maharashtra.* 1987 Cri. L.J. 743 (Bom).
4. *C. Jagadeeswar* v. *State of A.P.* 1988 Cri. L.J. 549 (A.P.).
5. *Supra* note 1.

Life is a patchwork—here and there,
Scraps of pleasure and despair
Join together, hit or miss

Anne Bronaugh, Patchwork

Chapter 2

THE RIGHT TO LIVE, AND TO DIE

*H.D. Shourie**

I HAVE throughout maintained that my life is my own. I discharge all my responsibilities to the best of my capacity and capability, fulfilling the obligations and duties life imposes on me. I live now for others, dedicating all my energies to work. But, when it comes to the question of my life I hold and maintain that it is my life and I have the right to live, or not to live. In asserting this right I feel fully rational and logical.

It is contended that in law the State alone has monopo listic right over my life, the State alone can take life. I cannot accept this contention; in fact, I totally discard it.

It is welcome that the Supreme Court[1] has upheld that as an individual I alone have the right to my life. This is fundamental right, enshrined in Article 21 of the Constitution; the right to life, including the right to live with dignity, recognising that finer graces of human living make life worth living. In expounding on this right the Court has held that while there is the positive aspect of this fundamental right, the right to live, it also encompasses the inter-linked and connected right, the right not to live. This part of the judgement of the Supreme Court, which is now being talked about and written on all over the country, is a very welcome elucidation of a fact which was obvious but which needed to be spelt out. I

* Director, "Common Cause" (An organisation for ventilating common problems of the people) New Delhi.

will have occasion later to touch upon other features of this important judgement, but this particular feature is practically the most prominent for being highlighted. The Supreme Court has held in this judgement that provisions of Section 309 of the Indian Penal Code are violative of this fundamental right. When I have inalienable right to live, or not to live, there cannot and should not be any argument that I have committed an offence by attempting to end my life or in other words, to commit suicide. If I succeed in ending the life, that is the finale; if I fail, it is no business of the State to prosecute me for the attempt.

The offence covering attempt to commit suicide has been in the Indian Penal Code since the Code was enacted over hundred years ago. The offence provides for imposition of sentence of imprisonment, upto one year, or of fine, or both, on a person found guilty of this offence. The High Courts of Delhi and Bombay in recent years have castigated this provision, holding that it was violative of the fundamental rights enshrined in the Constitution. Delhi High Court went to the extent of quashing all proceedings pending u/s 309 of I.P.C. and ordering the acquittal of 119 persons who were being prosecuted in different cases. The Court pointed out the futility of creating criminal liability in suicide cases, and of dragging the prosecution for years when the victims have already had enough of misery and that prosecutions were only adding insult to injury.

It is good that this judgement of the Supreme Court goes in fact to remove Section 309 I.P.C. from the statute book. This should have been done long ago. The Law Commission of India, as long ago as 1971, had recommended the repeal of this provision, expressing the view that it was obviously a monstrous procedure to inflict further suffering on an individual who has found life already unbearable, his chances of happiness slender, who is willing to face pain and death in order to cease living. They expressed that it was a perverse legislation that a person whose life is altogether bitter should be subjected to further bitterness and degradation. This recommendation of the Law Commission was accepted by the Government of India. An Amending Bill was introduced in 1972. It passed through the Rajya Sabha. It could not pass through Lok Sabha because it was dissolved and the Bill lapsed. Since then the matter has languished. Government of India has now shown readiness to bring the Bill again for effecting the amendment.

It is really a praiseworthy and Herculean effort that the Supreme Court has made in examining all possible aspects of the problem for assessing whether the provision of Section 309 I.P.C. should be declared void. It posed before itself as many as 16 specific questions in relation to this matter. The first question was whether the fundamental right to life, guaranteed by Article 21 of the Constitution, has the implicit aspect in it that this right involved also the right not to live. Other questions included such as whether suicide is immoral, whether it is a non-religious act, whether it produces adverse sociological effects, whether it is against public policy, why is suicide committed, who commits suicide, how suicide prone person should be dealt with, and such like. On each of these questions the Judge went through the entire gamut of analysing the views, judicial pronouncements, and expositions.

It is a satisfying experience to go through the material that has been marshalled in relation to each of these questions. Dealing with the question relating to public policy, for instance, the Court has put before itself all pros and cons of the arguments that allowing persons to commit suicide would be against public policy which charges the State with the responsibility of preservation of human life. The concept of public policy, however, is contended to be varying and uncertain, a vague and unsatisfactory doctrine. Public policy is not capable of precise definition; restraint of liberty, commerce, or legal rights, destruction of justice or violation of a statute can be argued to be against public policy. Concept of public policy varies with changing economic needs, social customs and moral aspirations of the people. Public policy can vary with habits and fashions of the day; what is public policy in one region may not be in another. On these various grounds the Court held that it would be wrong to assert with any degree of definiteness that commission of suicide is against public policy.

Likewise, in examining the question whether suicide is immoral all the various aspects of law and its relationship to morals have been analysed. It is right to be law-abiding, but there might be times when it is not wrong to break the law. Civil Disobedience Movement of India shows that there was clash of law and morality. It is argued that human life has sanctity, and this is defaced when a person commits suicide. This view held ground in U.K. There were objections on the grounds of morality, but U.K. itself set the pace by enacting the Suicide Act of 1961. Whereas previously suicide was regarded as a serious felony, requiring burial in a public highway and forfeiture of properties of the deceased, the Suicide Act of 1961 laid down that suicide was no longer to be regarded as an offence.

Factors or circumstances which lead to suicide have found special mention in this Supreme Court judgement. Causes can be various; economic, religious, socio-economic status, exasperations, fury, frustrations, revolution; feeling of burden, torture and sadness; loss of employment, reverse of fortune, misery due to illness, family trouble, thwarted love. Suicide knows no barriers of race, religion, caste or sex. In fact, there is complete secularisation of suicide. Persons from all religions and regions have succumbed to commit or attempt it. As many as 60,000 people are stated to commit suicide in one year in this country.

Main consideration is how the suicide prone persons should be dealt with. Do they deserve prosecution because they have failed? The Court has unequivocally said in the judgement that the answer to this question should be "No". Take some examples cited by the Court. Twenty persons committed suicide in Tamil Nadu on being distressed by the prolonged illness of the then Chief Minister Mr. Ramachandran. Should they have been prosecuted if their attempt had failed? Should a woman who attempts suicide because she has been raped be prosecuted? Would it not be adding grievous insult to compel her to face ignominy of undergoing an open trial exhibiting details of sexual violence which otherwise may be known only to a few?

This entire matter has now assumed wider dimension. It is not restricted merely to the question of declaration of suicide being not an offence or deletion of Section 309 of the Indian Penal Code. It has in recent years got closely linked with that of assisted suicide, passive euthanasia as well as active euthanasia. In any case euthanasia is not unrelated to the act of committing suicide. Suicide is not an offence; giving consent for termination of life should also not be an offence. The subject is now being widely debated in various countries and strong attitudes are developing in favour of euthanasia.

This attitude is gaining ground due to emergence of certain major developments. Population in every country is ageing, more so in the developed countries, though the developing countries are also not lagging behind. There are now more people alive above the limit of the life span of 72; many surviving beyond this limit. Advancements of medical science have placed instruments and facilities within reach; these help to prolong life. Previously death came when a person stopped breathing; now cardiopulmonary resuscitation and mechanical ventilators and respirators prolong life beyond what could have ever been previously conceived.

Advances in medical science and technology have particularly brought this matter to the fore. Question being asked is whether it is right to continue life-sustaining medical treatment in cases where all hope has extinguished, whether wishes of a person yet competent to exercise judgement, and the wishes previously expressed before lapsing into incapacity of exercising judgement, be respected and complied with in terminating life. These and many other similar questions have arisen in many countries. Some specific cases have captured the public imagination of these countries. There was the tragic case of 21-year Karen Ann Quinlan.[2] She collapsed during a party, ceased breathing for nearly 15 minutes, was rushed to hospital, placed on a respirator to restore breathing; during this interval she suffered irreversible brain damage and went into "persistent vegetative state" with no prospect of recovery. Her tormented parents petitioned the courts at various levels to allow the girl to die with "grace and dignity" and eventually the life sustaining equipment was allowed to be removed. There is the other case of 25-year old Nancy Cruzan[3] who met a serious car accident, was taken for dead, was revived by cardiopulmonary resuscitation but her brain had remained without oxygen for 12/14 minutes. She lapsed into state of unconsciousness which has lasted for over seven years.

She is stated to have often expressed, before the accident, that if she ever was reduced to vegetative state she should be allowed to die, but the courts, which were petitioned by the parents, declined to allow removal of life-sustaining equipment on the grounds that the patient had been rendered incompetent. The girl has laid for years in unconscious condition, suspended between life and death.† Latest, out of thousands, is that of Jacquiline Onassis, previously Jacquiline Kennedy, who passed away recently, with cancer having spread to her liver and brain, declining any extra-ordinary measures for prolongation of life, based on a living will executed by her.

Numerous persons in various parts of the world are presently lying in a "persistent vegetative state". In U.S.A. alone the number is estimated to be 10,000. Advances in medical technology have brought about conditions wherein they continue to remain suspended near death but not allowed to cross the threshold. In such cases of terminally ill persons, with no hope of recovery, adoption of procedures of passive euthanasia are being forcefully advocated. Active euthanasia is taken to be a criminal offence, but increasingly it too is being tolerated in practice. Practice prevailing in the Netherlands is particularly important in this connection. Physicians in the Netherlands who perform active euthanasia, actually helping the process of dying, are not prosecuted if they follow certain guidelines. These guidelines include: there should be an explicit and repeated request by the patient which leaves no reason for doubt concerning his desire to die; mental and physical suffering of the patient must be very severe with no prospect of relief; decision of patient is well informed and free; all other options for the patient have been exhausted. Increasingly people are relying on executing "Living Wills", authorising their surrogates to petition for removal of life-sustaining devices in the event of becoming terminally ill.

Certain individuals have emerged on the scene and have taken bold initiatives to propagate the concept of euthanasia, including also active euthanasia where circumstances necessitate it. Derek Humphry, who has set up the Hemlock Society and last year wrote "Final Exit" which immediately became the best seller, and Jack Keborkian, who has not hesitated to adopt aggressive procedures for termining life in cases of terminally ill patients and has even faced indictment for homicide, have in U.S.A. set the agenda for debate on this important subject.

These developments in various parts of the world have opened up new and vast vistas on this complex question of the right to live, and the right to die. India has had a long history, of illustrious personages who decided to terminate life, of the path they showed to rise above the trammels of earthy existence. Against the background of this long history of India's essays in this field, and amidst the widespread debate on various aspects of euthanasia, this Supreme Court judgement, holding the provisions of Section 309 of the Indian Penal Code regarding attempt to suicide to be void in law, is hopefully the beginning of initiatives for ultimate acceptance of assisted suicide, passive and active, subject to thorough safeguards against misuse, within the ambit of jurisprudence.

END NOTES

1. *P. Rathinam/Nagabhushan Patnaik* v. *Union of India* J.T. 1994(3) SC 392.
2. In *re Quinlan*, 355 A 2nd 647 (1976).
3. *Cruzan* v. *Director of Health Deptt*; 110's. ct 2841 (1990).

† *Editor's note*: A fresh hearing was held in the Missouri Courts where Cruzan doctors agreed that continuing like this would be a living hell for her that withdrawal was the right thing to do. The Missouri Court permitted withdrawal and Hancy Cruzan died soon thereafter. (See Andrew H. Malcolm, "Judge Allows feeding-tube Removal". N.Y. Times 15.12.1990, p. 10.)

Life's all getting and giving,
I've only myself to give.
What shall I do for a living?
I've only one life to live.
End it? I'll not find another.
Spend it? But how shall I best?
Sure the wise plan is to live like a man
And Luck may look after the rest.

Rudyard Kipling, The Wishing-Caps

Chapter 3

SUICIDE AND LIFE INSURANCE

*P.M. Bakshi**

THE TOPIC of suicide is capable of being approached from a variety of facets. The discussion may start on the plane of religion and morals, but is bound to touch the fringes of the law. When one says that it has got certain points of interaction with the law, one need not confine the study or discussion to the field of criminal law. Attempt to commit suicide has ceased to be an offence in most countries. In a few countries, while it is still on the statute book, the law is hardly being enforced. In India, recently, the Supreme Court[1] has declared Section 309 of the Indian Penal Code (attempt to commit suicide) as unconstitutional. But even where attempt to commit suicide has ceased to be an offence, certain questions will still survive, particularly in the field of civil law. In this field, the effect of suicide on life insurance has been an interesting topic which fills the law reports and academic literature.

For understanding the significance of the relationship between suicide and life insurance, one should have an idea of the historical background and of the content of life insurance policy. Suicide may be defined as the intentional destruction of oneself by a human being. In English law, suicide by a person who was sane and who had reached the age of discretion was a common law crime, and the punishment was burial in the highway, with a stake through the body of the

* Director, Indian Law Institute.

offender and forfeiture of all the goods of the offender to the Crown.[2] In fact, the consequence of forfeiture of goods in this and other cases was one of the circumstances which accounted for the utility of the office of Coroner, who was entrusted with the function of investigating into unnatural deaths. The question has also been debated whether suicide was a form of murder or whether it was a crime separate from murder. There is at least one author who takes the former view.[3]

In the United States, the question has been discussed whether suicide (even assuming that it is not an offence) is still an unlawful act. Apart from this, there are criminal law problems relating to suicide which concern the criminal liability of (1) one who unsuccessfully attempts to commit suicide, causing harm to no one else; (2) one whose unsuccessful attempts kills or injures someone else—a would-be rescuer or innocent bystander; and (3) one who persuades or aids or forces another to commit a successful suicide.[4]

Coming to the field of insurance, the law of life insurance (which is largely non-statutory) recognises certain express and implied conditions. Implied conditions are prescribed by law or by custom or by the nature of the contract of insurance. Express conditions are those which the parties agree to incorporate in the policy. For a long time, (subject to the general law of contracts), it has been settled that the parties are free to insert such conditions. In *Braunstein* v. *Accidental Death Insurance Co.*,[5] Lord Blackburn observed that the parties may make what they please a condition precedent, though he added that it must be shown that the parties so intended. It follows, that if a life insurance policy specifically excludes death consequential on suicide from the zone of risks covered by the policy, then such a condition would be valid, and it is a clear case in which right to recover under the policy would be excluded.

What is the position if there is no express condition against suicide? It would appear, on principle, that even in such a case recovery would be barred on the basis of an implied condition. While a person insuring himself under a life insurance policy does not undertake that he will not embark upon hazardous activities, he does seem to undertake that he will not intentionally put an end to his life. On the one hand, as was observed by Chief Baron Pollock in *Baxendale* v. *Harley*.[6] "If a person who insures his life goes in a balloon, that does not vitiate the policy". The reason is that there is no implied condition that the insured person shall not do anything which may endanger his life.[7] (1917) (33 T.L.R. 430). On the other hand, however, intentional destruction of the subject-matter of the policy by the person insured cannot supply an occasion for claiming recovery because a party to a contract cannot be allowed, to recover (by way of "insurance"), where he brings into existence the very event regarding which he is insured. Generally speaking, a person takes out the insurance because of the uncertainty of the future event which is not dependent on his volition. It is a travesty of language to speak of insurance, when the conduct in question is a deliberate one. It would therefore seem to follow, that the very concept of coverage against risk of an event, dependent either on unforeseen circumstances or on the will of a third person rules out recovery under a life insurance policy in case of suicide. There is a large number of decisions holding that recovery is not permissible in the case of suicide under a life insurance policy.[8]

In England, it is a crime for a person to aid, abet, counsel or procure the suicide of another person, under Section 2(1), Suicide Act, 1961 which abolished the main offence of suicide. It has also been held in England that at the Coroner's inquest, suicide must be strictly proved and it is not a verdict which ought to be reached as being the most likely cause of death.[9]

In American law, attempted suicide is a crime in some jurisdictions, not in others. Some jurisdictions in the United States hold an attempted suicide which kills an innocent bystander or a would-be rescuer to be murder; a few jurisdictions hold it to be manslaughter; others do not consider it to be a crime. But it would appear that even in American law, recovery would not be allowed under a life insurance policy if there is a deliberate destruction of life by the very person who is insured. Juristically, one can regard the situation as analogous to the situations in which the maxim *ex turpi causa non oritur actio* operates, that is to say, an action cannot arise out of a base cause. The point to make is, that the removal of the offence of attempt to commit suicide from the operation of the substantive criminal law, as such, may not necessarily have an impact on those doctrines of the law which justify themselves on certain implicit ethical principles. In this context, one has to take into account the fact that conduct may be approved by the law, disapproved by the law, though not specifically treated as illegal, or regarded as illegal by the law, though not treated as an offence and finally, expressly punished by the law which constitutes it an offence. An act of suicide may not fall in the last category and in the first category, but it can still fall within the second or the third category. One here enters the uncharted waters of the policy of the law. To take a leap from non-punishability by the law to positive approval of the conduct in question by the law is a quantum jump which may not be taken in every case. We have a Latin maxim in these words—*Lex est sanctio sancta, jubens honesta, et prohibens contraria*. (Law is a sacred sanction, commanding what is right, and prohibiting the contrary.) This maxim, like most maxims of the law, only illuminates a facet of reality. One should also remember another maxim, namely, *Lex est dictamen rationis*. (The common law will judge according to the law of nature and the public good.)

END NOTES

1. *P. Rathinam/Nagabhushan Patnaik* v. *Union of India*. J.T. 1994 (3) SC 392.
2. See *Hales* v. *Petit* Plowd. 253, 260-65, 75 Eng. Rep. 387, 397–400 (B. 1565); Burnett v. People 204, III 208, 222, 68 N.E. 505, 510 (1903).
3. See Mikell, "Is Suicide Murder", 3 *Columbia Law Review* 379 (1903) cited by Faye and Scot, *Criminal Law* 568 (1972).
4. See Larremore, "Suicide and the Law" *17 Harv. L. Rev.* 331 (1904).
5. (1861) 31 L.J.Q.B. 17.
6. (1859) 28 *Law Journal Exchequer* 236: 157 E.R. 913.
7. *Duckworth* v. *Scottish Widows' Fund Life Assurance Society* (1917) 33 T.L.R. 430.
8. *Beresford* v. *Royal Insurance* (1938) AC 586 (H.L.) is one such example.
9. *R. City of London Coroner* (1975) I.W.L.R. 1310; *Kirkham* c. *Chief Constable of the Greater Manchester Police* (1990) 3 All E.R. 246.

Chapter 4

THE RIGHT TO DIE: INDIAN PERSPECTIVE

*Bal Krishna**

AT THE present time, a "right to die" has been proclaimed by many organisations and individuals. There is a Society for the Right to Die, many states do have "right-to-die" or "death-with-dignity" statutes, and increasing numbers of individuals have filled out advance directives for health care, so-called "living wills", outlining, sometimes in great details, ways in which their right to die should be honoured when they are terminally ill or irreversibly comatose.

However, the Supreme Court in a recent judgement[1] dismissed a plea to transmute the "right to die" into a "right to be killed by a physician or any other person" if a person is terminally ill or otherwise. In striking down Section 309 of the Indian Penal Code (I.P.C.) which makes "attempt to commit suicide" a penal offence, the Supreme Court of India has come to the rescue of those who live a dreadful life and suffer from mental and physical agony and incurable diseases and have lost all hope of redemption. Now the law grants them the liberty and the right to die of their own will, accord and desire and if they fail in their attempt they cannot be prosecuted.

Of course, the Court made it clear that the "right to die" does not mean a "right to be killed" by a third person, because under the law, the abetting of suicide is still punishable by imprisonment. Secondly, right to die is again subject to

* M.Sc., LL.B., Legal Correspondent, *The Hindustan Times*, New Delhi.

other laws of the land. For example, under Commission of Sati (Prevention) Act, 1987, the widow's right to die either of her own will or under compulsion on the pyre of her husband is prohibited.

In this background, let us examine what is the attitude of Indian religious communities to this alleged right to die? Can the Hindu ethical traditions support death with dignity? What is the response of Hindu communities to the ethical dilemmas raised by modern medical technology that can starve off death without restoring health for days, weeks, months, and even years.

According to the Hindu Vedantic philosophy, death is not the end of life. It is only the *sthula sharira* (physical body), that dies. It is the *sukshma sharira* (the astral body), that does not perish with the death of the body. The *sukshma sharira* is very complex, consisting, among other things, of the life breath of vital principle, mind, *buddhi* (intelligence), and, some philosophers believe, of *ahankaras* (false egoes) also. The impressions of past *karmas* (thoughts and deeds) remain in the *sukshma sharira* or astral body, and are retained even after death and goes to *bhuvarloka antariksha* (the astral plane) and then to *svargaloka* (heaven or the mental plane). The astral body then disintegrates and the components are merged in the Ocean of Energy with the Eternal *Parama Brahma* (The Supreme Creator). Thereafter they return by the will of God to another physical body, and the individual is reborn on this earth in accordance with that person's deeds and *karmas*.

It would not be wrong to say that there is an imperishable ocean of energy which is *Parama Brahma*. It is infinite and self-luminous, free from births and deaths. We all are droplets or lumps or only parts of that great ocean of energy. This droplet of energy enters our bodies which live a life, act, and enjoy. When the body becomes unfit to live, the droplet of energy leaves the body and enters another. This is called "transmigration of the soul." In other words, when the soul enters the body we call it birth; when it leaves the body we say it is death. It is a continuous process. In Bhagwad Gita, the Lord Krishna says, "Just as a person casts off worn-out garments and puts on others that are new, even so does the embodied soul cast off worn out bodies and take on others that are new."

Can one in these circumstances meet death of one's own will and accord? Has one a right to die? Can a medical practitioner, friend, or family member assist one in meeting death? Do custom, ethics, or religion permit it? Is it a part of tort and human rights of citizens to die of their own will? Is it or is it not a crime with legal punishment? Should the law of the land permit it?

According to Vedantic philosophy, the *Parama Brahma* created the human being. God is present in the soul of the human being. Life is offered to us by him in order for us to offer obeisance to God, to obey *dharma*, to perform duties that are assigned to us, and to tread the path of righteousness. God is the material cause and instrumentality of all joys, happiness, woes, sorrows, deeds and *karmas* of humanity. Just as He gave life to us, He takes it away from us as well. He is the creator as well as the doer and the destroyer of this body.

Lord Krishna in Bhagwad Gita affirms the Vedantic philosophy: Having come to me, says Lord Krishna, these great souls do not get back to rebirth, the place of sorrows, pain, non-eternal, for they have reached the highest perfection and bliss. He further says that for the one that is born, death is certain; and for the one that has died, birth is certain. Since it is inevitable, one should not grieve. Birth and death are two ends of life.

This takes us to two different philosophies of death. One asks: if life is given and taken away by the will of God alone and we only obey His commands, do we possess the right to do away with our lives at our will whatever may be our circumstances? We cannot desire death deliberately even if death is inevitable. The other view asks: If the entire universe and all living beings are nothing but the manifestations of God Himself and if the world is not only the body of God but His remainder, if we are only a droplet of energy of the great ocean of energy and will finally merge with that ocean of energy, if we arise from Him and upon death return to Him again, and if God is in us and we are a part of God, then where is the wrong in meeting death of our own free will and desire at any time we like? Since we will then merge with the Almighty, how can it be an act of sin or crime worth punishment?

The great saints, seers and sages of India from time immemorial have been following the latter law of religious philosophy. They beckoned, welcomed, and met death at will in the later part of their ascetic lives by taking *samadhi* (complete absorption in God-consciousness) to attain peace and *moksha* (salvation). Many of them were even blessed with the greatest human virtue of *ichcha mrityu* (commanding death at will). They could not be killed or die otherwise. They were idolised out of reverence and obeisance was made to them. Such saints were worshipped as gods.

In the Mahabharata we find that after the victory of good over evil and of *dharma* (righteousness) over *adharma* (sin), and after being freed from obligations and duties to society and the kingdom, both the ancestors and the guru of the *Pandavas* and *Kauravas* beckoned to death and, having *ichcha mrityu*, voluntarily died. Many others met death of their own will, including Lord Rama and his brothers who, after fulfilling their duties and obligations in life, voluntarily gave their lives by taking *samadhi* in the river Saryu in Ayodhya. There were no laws to restrict a saint, seer, or ascetic from taking *samadhi* at will. On the contrary, the practice had religious sanctions. They had the right to die of their own will.

From time immemorial also, the Aryan women in the country had the religious, moral and social sanction to end their lives on the funeral pyres of their husbands (*sati*). *Sati* was a consequence and manifestation of the extreme love of the widow for her dead husband or of the desire for the bliss of paradise. It was sometimes committed out of the desire for salvation of the soul or for special prestige. The spiritual significance of *sati* was stressed in the ancient religious books of the Hindus. *Sati* was said to be a duty and also a right for a Hindu widow to die upon her husband's death. She was idolised and worshipped for committing sati. Religious fairs and *yajnas* (sacrifices) were annually or periodically held at such places and *samadhis*. The belief was that if wives died with their husbands the two would never be separated in the heavens or in other lives and rebirths to come.

According to *Parashar Smriti* and *Brahma* and *Gurar Puranas*, if the widow dies on the funeral pyre of her deceased husband, she develops the power to carry her husband away from hell and to live with him in the heavens with all pleasures and happiness for three-and-a-half crore (35 million) years. It is further said that she will be respected and worshipped like Sanyasin Arundhati, the wife of the great saint Rajasshi Vashisth. Sanyasin Arundhati met her death by sati on the funeral pyre of her husband, and, by her powers and the virtues of *sati*, she can now been seen shining like a star near the Galaxy of the Seven Stars.

However, there was one exception to this rule. Widows who were pregnant at the time of their husband's death or who had infant children were prohibited from committing *sati*. A *Kshatriya* widow invariably committed sati upon her husband's death. If a king was defeated in war and there was a chance that the women of the palace would be molested or not respected, the womenfolk were permitted to commit suicide by jumping into a fire within the palace in order to save their honour and chastity. *Sati* was a must for *Kshatriya* (the then ruling class) widows or women during war, but it was not universal for all. It was optional for widows of other communities, such as *Brahmins*, *Vaishyas* and *Shudras*. They could either commit *sati* or live a very pious and ascetic life with restrictions as prescribed in religious books. In certain states, they could even remarry in special circumstances, but only their husbands' younger brother. This option for widows, however, came into vogue later as a result of the impact of Buddhism on Hindu society in India. Many such women turned Buddhist after the deaths of their husbands, to save themselves from cruelty and torture.

Another reason for this right of the widow to die was the law of inheritance prevalent in those days among the Hindus. In Bengal, according to the *Dayabhaga* school of inheritance, the widow had rights to her deceased husband's property which barred the claims of his father, mother, brothers, sisters and daughters. This custom inspired the other members of the family to compel the widow to die by committing *sati* in order to prevent her from being the sole successor. In states, where the *Mitakshara* school of law prevailed, however, the surviving widow's rights in her husband's property were circumscribed. It enjoined property distribution among all the successors of the deceased, of whom the widow would be only one. In these states the practice of sati or the widow dying with her husband was a rare phenomenon.

It was one of the practices that scandalised the British from earliest days. Nevertheless from the very first, they adopted the policy of non-interference with the religious and social customs of the natives. According to V.N. Datta, the rite of *sati* most probably received its first official mention in 1787, when Sir Charles Malet, the Resident at Poona, enclosed an account by Mr Cruso of a *sati* which took place in Poona in 1786. Thereafter, from time to time, a few magistrates in the Bengal Presidency reported their success in persuading young widows to desist from committing *sati*. They also continued to ask for rules for their guidance, especially when the woman was being coerced into immolating herself after being stupefied with drugs. The Government of Fort William approved of the successes, admonished them to use only persuasion and did not give any specific directions.

In 1805, Lord Wellesley, the Governor-General of India, formally asked the Court of Nizamat Adalat whether sati could be abolished, administering intoxicants be prevented to widows and women who were not capable of judging for themselves. A Hindu was consulted by the law officers of the Nizamat Adalat who replied that *sati* was founded on the religious texts of Hindus and was expressly stated in their law. There were, however, certain circumstances during which the woman could not commit *sati*, namely, if she was pregnant, under puberty, mother of an infant, unless someone offered to look after it, in a state of uncleanliness, i.e., menstruating and stupefied with drugs.

Most important, the *sati* had to be entirely voluntary, which required that the woman should have taken the decision completely on her own without any external influence. Though this opinion was received in 1805, the government did not formulate its policy on this practice until 1812 when it declared by a circular that like all other religious practices, sati should be allowed where it was countenanced by their religion and prevented where it was forbidden. The distinction was thus made between legal and illegal *sati*, however cautiously. The government defined a *sati* as illegal when the woman was under compulsion, intoxicated, pregnant or had a child under three years whose nurture was not undertaken by another.

Finally, Lord Bentinck outlawed sati in 1829, but the practice continued, especially in Rajasthan. Recently, in 1987, when a newly married woman named Roop Kanwar committed *sati* in Rajasthan on the pyre of her husband, a great hue and cry was raised by the womenfolk and the people in general. The country was badly shaken. The result was that on January 3, 1988, the Commission of Sati (Prevention) Act, 1987 was enacted in the country which makes sati as crime. The attempting, abetting, and glorification of sati have all been declared punishable by a range of penalties that could include life imprisonment or even the death.

In 1860, the Government of India modified the Indian Penal Code (I.P.C.). Under Section 309 of the I.P.C., the attempt to commit suicide and under Section 306, the abetting of suicide were made punishable by imprisonment. The act of committing suicide, when successful, is not and cannot be regarded as a crime in India, but if unsuccessful it is a crime punishable under the law. In a case reported in 1914, a division bench of the Allahabad High Court held that in a case in which some people gave a widow ghee which she poured over her husband's funeral pyre and also upon herself, such accused persons were guilty of abetting suicide.

In another case reported in 1919,[2] the same High Court held that, where a woman driven almost frantic by the pains of prolonged labour during childbirth attempted to take her own life and as a result her infant was born dead, she was guilty of attempting to commit suicide. But in another case reported in 1934,[3] it was held by the erstwhile Punjab High Court that, if a person on account of family discord, destitution, loss of a dear relation, or other cause of a like nature overcomes the instict of self-preservation and decides to take his or her own life; it is not necessary to inflict sentence of imprisonment on that person under Section 309 of I.P.C.

Gandhiji once observed: "Death is our friend, the truest of friends. He relieves us from agony. I do not want to die of a creeping paralysis of my faculties—a defeated man." The English poet William Ernest Hentley wrote: "I am the master of my fate, I am the captain of my soul."

Despite the above, Hamlet's dilemma of "To be or not to be" faces many a soul in times of distress, agony and suffering, when the question asked is: "To die or not to die." If the decision be to die and the same is implemented to its fructification resulting in death, that is the end of the matter. The dead is relieved of the agony, pain and suffering and no evil consequences known to our law follow. But if the person concerned be unfortunate to survive, the attempt to commit suicide may see him behind the bars, as the same is punishable under Section 309 of I.P.C.

In 1987, the Bombay High Court in *Maruti Shripati Dubal* v. *State of Maharashtra*[4] struck down Section 309 as violative of Article 21 of the Constitution. According to the Court this article confers a positive right to live which carries with it the negative right not to live. In this connection it has been first stated that the fundamental rights are to be read together as held in *R.C. Cooper* v. *Union of India.*[5] In this case the Court observed that the freedom of speech and expression includes freedom not to speak and to remain silent. Likewise the freedom of business and occupation, includes freedom not to do business.

Notice was also taken by the Court of the various causes which lead people to commit suicide. These being mental diseases and imbalances, unbearable physical ailments, affliction by socially dreaded diseases, physically disabling ailments which make a person handicapped, the loss of all senses or of desire for the pleasures of any of the senses, extremely cruel or unbearable conditions of life making it painful to live, a sense of shame or disgrace or a need to defend one's honour or sheer loss of interest in life or disenchantment with it, or a sense of fulfilment of the purpose for which one was born with nothing more left to do or to achieve and genuine urge to quit the world at the proper moment.

The Court thereafter stated that in India different forms of suicide are known. These being: *Jauhars* (mass suicides or self-immolation) of ladies from the royal palaces to avoid being dishonoured by the enemies; *sati* (self-immolation by the widow on the burning pyre of her deceased husband) *samadhi* (termination of one's life by self-restraint on breathing); *prayopaveshan* (starvation unto death); and *atmarpana* (self-sacrifice). It was also observed that many saints and sarvants in India have immolated themselves in the past and do so even today by one method or the other. The Indian society has not only disapproved of the practice but has also eulogised and commend such people. It may be pointed out that the Court made a distinction between "suicide" and "mercy-killing", so also, between suicide and aiding or abetting the same.

The High Court held Section 309 as violative of Article 15 also mainly because of two reasons. First, which act, or acts or series of acts will constitute attempt to suicide, and it is difficult to draw the exact line—some attempts may be serious while others non-serious. It was stated that in fact philosophers, moralists and sociologists have divergent views as to what constituted suicide. The want of plausible definition or even guidelines made Section 309 arbitrary as per the Court. Another reason given was that Section 309 treats all attempts to commit suicide by the same measure without referring to the circumstances in which attempts are made.

The first of the aforesaid reasons was not sound according to a latest judgement of the Supreme Court in *P. Rathinam*[6] because whatever differences there may be as to what constitutes suicide, there was no doubt according to the apex Court that suicide was intention of taking of one's life.

Of course, there still exists difference among suicide researchers as to what constitute suicidal behaviour, for example, whether narcotic addiction, chronic alcoholism, heavy smoking, reckless driving, other risk taking behaviours are suicidal or not. It may also be that different methods are adopted in committing suicide, for example, use of firearms, poison, over dose of drugs, hanging, inhalation of gas, drowning, and so on. Further, on a prosecution being launched it is always open to an accused to take the plea that his act did not constitute suicide whereupon the Court would decide this aspect.

The apex Court had also rejected the finding of the Bombay High Court that attempt to commit suicide violates

Article 14 of the Constitution. Justice B.L. Hansaria who delivered the judgement pointed out that Section 309 has only provided the maximum sentence which is up to one year. It provides for imposition of fine only as a punishment.

The Bombay High Court judgement was also criticised by some thinkers. The broad points of their criticism were: suicide is an act against religion; it is immoral; it produces adverse sociological effects, it is against public policy, it damages monopolistic power of the State as State alone can take life; and it would encourage aiding and abetting of suicide and may even lead to "Constitutional Cannibalism." The Supreme Court in its judgement dealt with all these points at length.

The Law Commission of India in its 42nd Report (1971) recommended repeal of Section 309 being of the view that this penal provision is "harsh and unjustifiable". In taking this view, the Law Commission quoted the following observations made by H. Romilly Fedden in "Suicide":

> "It seems a monstruous procedure to inflict further suffering on even a single individual who has already found life so unbearable, his chances of happiness so slender, that he has been willing to face pain and death in order to cease living. That those for whom life is altogether bitter should be subjected to further bitterness and degradation seems perverse legislation."

In recent times Acharya Vinobha Bhave, the great disciple of Mahatma Gandhi, having grown old and being satisfied with his service to humanity, thought it was time for him to die. In 1983 he voluntarily stopped taking food, medicine and water. Persuasions by Indian leaders including Indira Gandhi, then Prime Minister, did not dissuade him. He died of his own wish on the auspicious Dipawali day. His act was not regarded as suicide; no criminal action was taken by the State to protect his life.

The other recent case was that of Justice Shashi Kant Varma, retired Chief Justice of the Allahabad High Court. He was an eminent jurist and a sportsman endowed with vigour and strength even at age of 70. He had all the pleasures and blessings in life with health, wealth, fame, and children occupying high positions. He had no unfulfilled ambitions and was fully satisfied and relieved of his responsibilities and obligations. In 1988 he was treated for cancer and recovered. He felt, however, that life no longer held charm for him and was no longer worth living. He decided he had the right to die. One fine evening he retired to his room and fired a shot into his head from his own pistol, thus voluntarily ending his life. It was not a sin or a crime.

The latest case is that of Amrit Ram Shastri Vaidacharya, an eminent Sanskrit scholar of Delhi. At 74 years of age, he felt he had enjoyed life well and in old age was facing problems that took away the joy of life. One fine evening (September 23, 1993) he went to take a dip in river Yamuna, took *jal samadhi* and gave up his life.

In recent years, the Government of India has permitted human beings during their lifetime to donate their kidneys and, after death, their eyes, and other vital organs for the benefit of those whose organs have failed. The right to donate parts of human body is an effective and meaningful legal right in the modern world. The process of transplantation of vital organs is hazardous. Donors may lose their lives during the process or afterwards as a result of the donation, yet the government has permitted it. If this can be a legal right, why can we not have right to do away with our entire body and life?

There is another law called the Medical Termination of Pregnancy Act, 1971 which legalise the murder of a child in the womb at the will of the mother or her guardian. Similarly, explanation I of Section 3(2)(b) of the Act provides for legalising abortion for a woman or girl who becomes pregnant as a result of rape. The law permits the termination of such pregnancy if she so desires, partly perhaps because an unmarried pregnant girl or woman, even being raped, will not be accepted by society. Such a girl or woman may not be allowed to lead a decent life with dignity and honour. On the other hand, she will most likely be an object of hatred. Now the law does permit such a woman to die of her own will.

There are cases in which men found guilty of murder, dacoity and other serious criminal offences have been sentenced to death, but for one reason or another the infliction of the death sentence has been postponed for years. The condemned are thus made to languish for years in isolated cells, segregated from other prisoners and from their family members and friends. The fear of death hangs over them for years and causes great mental tension and anguish. Yet the law in India does not permit them to meet their own death as a result of their own will. Because they are criminals they have no right to die, although in similar circumstances of injury to mental and physical health a woman is permitted to end a pregnancy and kill an unborn child.

The apex Court judgement has come to the rescue of those who live a dreadful life and suffer from mental and physical agony and incurable diseases and have lost all hope for redemption. The law laid down by the Supreme Court grant some of the people the liberty and the right to die of their own will, accord and desire.

END NOTES

1. *P. Rathinam/Nagabhushan Patnaik* v. *Union of India,* J.T. 1994 (3) SC 392.
2. *Emperor* v. *Mulia* (1919), 20 Cri. L.J. 395 (ALL).
3. *Barkar* v. *Emperor,* Cri. L.J. 682 (Lab.) 1934.
4. 1987, Cri. L.J. 743.
5. AIR 1970, SC 1318.
6. *Supra* note 1.

Chapter 5

THE VERDICT

It closes one question, but opens some more.

*Niti Paul Mehta**

THE PROBLEM of suicide is not new. Its roots lie buried in the mists of antiquity. It finds mention in the Vedas, the Puranas and the Bible. Enlightened minds, concerned with the problems of human behaviour, have in all ages sought to have insights into the intricate and complex processes which go on in the hidden recesses of the minds of suicide prone personalities. Among the thinkers, philosophers and intellectuals in whose writings we find a mention of the subject are Plato, Cicero, Voltaire, Sir Thomas More, Francis Bacon, David Hume, H.G. Wells and George Bernard Shaw. Unfortunately, society did not always treat such persons with sympathy. In most societies they were treated with savage cruelty.

Modern research and studies, especially those conducted in the West in the past half of the century, have unravelled many mysteries and given us better understanding of the working of the minds of the suicide prone persons. But most of this knowledge is available only in generalised terms. There are still large unexplored areas, and why people commit suicide still remains a mystery in many ways. Each case of suicide has its own context and can be understood in the light of that particular context or situation alone. Each suicide also reveals some new aspect of the problem.

* Freelance Journalist, Educationist and Commentator,.

Despite this growing knowledge and understanding of abnormal, deviant human behaviour, both law and society have failed to control or check in any meaningful way the ever increasing number of suicides. More people now actually commit suicide or attempt to commit suicide than they did at any given time in history.

According to the figures released by the National Crime Records Bureau and quoted in the Press 80,149 persons committed suicide in 1992. For 1981 the figure was 40,245. According to conservative estimates 100 persons make a bid to commit suicide every hour. But these official statistics reveal only the tip of the iceberg when unreported or hushed up number of suicides and attempted suicides are also taken into account. Self-destruction is, thus, fast becoming one of the major causes of death in this country. Judging by the alarming rate of growth in the incidence of suicides, the number of suicide-related deaths could be anywhere in the range of 1,00,000 and 1,50,000 by the turn of the century.

What is it that compels a person to commit suicide? Why are attempts at 'self-destruction' on the increase? Answers to these uneasy questions are not easy concerned as they are with the often unpredictable part of human behaviour. In some cases where the persons committing suicide leave notes behind them, the circumstances leading to the fatal step might give some insight into the main cause(s) which compelled them to commit suicide. But in most cases even these notes are either vague or impersonal like the ones which begin "No one is to be blamed...", or "The world will not miss me...". The only fact that the world comes to know is that a suicide has been committed or it has been attempted. But research has established that there are certain things which have a definite role in creating a situation in which a person might seriously think of ending his life.

There are periods in every person's life when he feels depressed and distressed. Tensions pile up, conflicts multiply, frustrations overwhelm, the faculty to think clearly gets impaired, the mind gets trapped in a groove and a state of ambivalence takes over. He loses touch with reality and finds the situation hopeless. He can see no way out, no light at the end of the tunnel. Under such circumstances, being not in a position to think rationally, he might overreact and contemplate committing suicide as the only way out. This state of ambivalence, when a person's mind is assailed by contrary thoughts is perhaps best illustrated by Hamlet's soliloquy:

> To be, or not to be: that is the question:
> Whether 'tis nobler in the mind to suffer
> The slings and arrows of outrageous fortune,
> Or to take arms against a sea of troubles,
> And by opposing end them? To die: to sleep;
> No more; and by a sleep to say we end
> The heart-ache and the thousand natural shocks
> That flesh is heir to, 'tis a consummation
> Devoutly to be wish'd. To die, to sleep;
> To sleep: perchance to dream: ay, there's the rub;
> For in that sleep of death what dreams may come
> When we have shuffled off this mortal coil,
> Must give us pause...

Virginia Woolf who committed suicide by drowning herself left this note behind for her husband: "I have a feeling I shall go mad. I cannot go on any longer in these terrible times. I hear voices and cannot concentrate on my work. I have fought against it but cannot fight any longer. I owe all my happiness to you but cannot go and spoil your life."

The note reveals a pathetic state of the mind of a person who is completely confused. She cannot think rationally. She finds herself completely down and out. She is unable to meet the challenge of living in those 'terrible times'. She cannot cope with the situation. She does not want to spoil her husband's life by continuing to live in that state of the mind. So she solves the problem by ending her life. That is how the mind of a suicidal person gets caught in a groove.

Economic problems, heavy losses in business, inability to cope with the fast competitive modern-day life, unemployment, failure, a mental sickness like depression or schizophrenia, loss of job, domestic conflicts/unhappiness, death of a loved one or some such other emotionally shattering experience, a feeling of loneliness or of being unwanted, a feeling that life has lost its purpose and has no meaning left in it, hostility towards others or towards one's own self or a deep rooted sense of having been wronged by the family or a friend or by a loved one or even by society, a feeling of being betrayed in love, social disgrace and humiliation as, for instance, suffered by a rape victim, or being terminally sick are some of the causes which singly or in combination might drive a person to commit suicide.

Human reactions vary. In a single given situation of stress one person might attempt to commit suicide while the same situation with the same amount of stress may not provoke the same reaction in another person. Persons who commit suicide are generally known to have lower levels of tension. Their inner controls are weak. They cannot bear many pressures or tensions of life. Most often such persons suffer from some kind of emotional or mental imbalance. Every person who attempts to commit suicide does it under an impulse which brings on a temporary fit of insanity. If there is one thing which comes out clearly in Virginia Woolf's suicide note quoted above is her abnormal, disturbed state of the mind which robbed her of her rationality and provoked her to overreact.

Reacting to the reports of his accidental death appearing in the Press, the American novelist, Ernest Hemingway, had written:

> "In all the obituaries, or almost all, it was emphasised that I had sought death all my life. Can anyone imagine that if a man sought death all his life, he could not have found her before the age of 54?
>
> It is one thing to be in the proximity of death, to know more or less what she is, and it is quite another thing to seek her. She is the most easy thing to find that I know of. You may find her through a minor carelessness, on a road with heavy traffic, you could find her in a bottle of Seconol, you could find her with any type of razor blade; you could find her in your own bathtub or you could find her by not being battlewise. If you have spent your life avoiding death as cagily as possible but, on the other hand,

taking no back-chat from her and studying her as you would a beautiful harlot who would put you soundly to sleep for ever with no problems and no necessity to work, you could be said to have studied her but not sought her."

This note clearly shows Hemingway's preoccupation or rather obsession with the idea of death. He was avoiding death but in 1961 he shot himself dead because he was suffering from a terminal illness. Despite his denial the idea of suicide might have been all along with him.

In most cases a person who commits suicide does not actually want to die. He even hopes till the last that some relative, some friend or some acquaintance would come to his rescue and save him. When, some years ago, a young doctor committed suicide by consuming an over-dose of sleeping pills in the hostel room of a Delhi Medical College, a colleague had expressed surprise at the fact that his body was found not in his own room but in the room of a friend.

There was actually nothing unusual about it. It only proved that this doctor did not want to die. He hoped that his friend, a doctor-colleague, might come to his room and discovering him in that condition, might take timely action and save him. But as it happens in most such cases, things did not go the way he had expected. By the time his friend came back to his room, it was already too late.

An attempt to commit suicide is, in fact, a desperate cry for attention, a strong plea for help. In many cases the suicide prone persons communicate their intention to commit suicide in clear terms. One person may express his intention before a friend another may ring up the police to say that he is going to commit suicide. Often they might even state the mode they would be adopting, indicating also the time and place of the intended fatal step. In Delhi crisis centres being run by voluntary organisations, like Sanjeevani and Sumaitri receive frequent stress calls from suicidal persons. According to one agency report Sumaitri alone receives around ten such calls a day.

According to *Today's Health Guide*, edited by Dr. W.W. Bauer, "Threats of suicide should always be taken seriously.

There is a tragic misconception that people who say they are going to kill themselves never do. Quite the contrary is true; most people who commit suicide have warned others before of their intentions. A threat of suicide is always a reason for taking immediate, preventive action."

When a person threatens to commit suicide he is actually sending out two signals. One of these is quite clear: his intention to take his own life. The other is implied in this threat itself. That signal is the real all important one but unfortunately it often gets overlooked. By threatening to commit suicide the person is pleading for help. He wants to live and expects his family and friends to come to his rescue and take steps to ensure that he does not succeed in his objective. He desperately needs counselling and emotional support and maybe psychiatric treatment.

The last 50 years have witnessed a marked change in the socio-legal as well as judicial attitudes all over the world towards the problem of suicide and suicide prone persons.

Persons who attempt to commit suicide are now looked upon as mentally or emotionally sick persons. They are social misfits. They suffer from some kind of inadequacies. In whatever light they may appear to others, they are an unfortunate lot. Persons who fail in their attempt to commit suicide undergo and tolerate unbearable agony, torment, ignominy and even social ostracization to a certain extent. These unfortunate persons do not deserve punishment but medical attention in the form of counselling and psychiatric treatment. Punishment in dealing with such cases is a negative approach which can prove neither curative nor corrective. In fact there are instances in which a person after going through the judicial process has once again attempted suicide and succeeded in killing himself. What he actually needs is positive psychotherapy. The basic fact is that a person who attempts to commit suicide has some problem which is too large for him to cope with. He needs help to come through it. His is not a law and order problem. Whether an attempt to commit suicide is considered a crime or not makes no difference to a person who is intent on committing suicide.

The first indication of a shift in judicial thinking in this country on the subject of suicide came when a Division Bench of the Delhi High Court in *State* v. *Sanjay Kumar*[1] observed: "The continuance of Section 309 I.P.C. is an anachronism unworthy of a human society like ours. Medical clinics for such social misfits certainly but police and prison never...Need is for a humane, civilised and socially oriented outlook and penology...No wonder so long as society refuses to face this reality its coercive machinery will invoke the provision like 309 I.P.C. which has no justification or right to continue to remain on the statute book."

In 1987 a Division Bench of Bombay High Court in *Maruti Shripati* v. *State of Maharashtra*[2] had held that Section 309 was "ultra vires being violative of Articles 14 and 21 of the Constitution and was therefore struck down."

However, a Division Bench of Andhra Pradesh High Court in *C. Jagadeeswer* v. *State of Andhra Pradesh*[3] held that the Section (309 I.P.C.) was valid as it did not offend any of the Articles (i.e., Articles 14 and 21 of the Constitution). The Bombay view was dissented to.

In its 42nd Report (1971) the Law Commission of India recommended the repeal of Section 309 I.P.C.

The recommendations made by the Law Commission were accepted by the Government of India. Consequently, I.P.C. (Ammendment) Bill 1972 was introduced in the Rajya Sabha to repeal Section 309 I.P.C. The Bill was referred to a Joint Committee of both the Houses. It was passed with some modifications by the Rajya Sabha in 1978. It was pending with the Lok Sabha when the House was dissolved in 1979 and the Bill lapsed.

As a logical conclusion to these ongoing legal and judicial developments the Supreme Court allowed the writ petitions filed in the case of *State* v. *Nagabhushan Patnaik*[4] and struck down Section 309 I.P.C. "as unconstitutional and hence void". It was held violative of Article 21 of the Constitution. The apex Court observed that "It (Section 309 I.P.C.) is a cruel and irrational provision, and it may result in punishing a person again (doubly) who has suffered agony and would be undergoing ignominy because of his failure to commit suicide."[5]

The learned Court also observed that "an act of suicide cannot be said to be against religion, morality and public policy, and an act of attempted suicide has no baneful effect on society. Further, suicide or attempt to commit suicide causes no harm to others, because of which State's interference with the personal liberty of the concerned persons is not called for."

Questions whether suicide is against religion or morality have been discussed in the verdict at some length. References have been made to Lord Rama and his brothers who ended their lives by taking *Jalasamadhi*, and Acharya Vinobha Bhave who ended his life by fasting himself to death. The apex Court has also quoted G.P. Tripathi who in his address to the World Congress on Law and Medicine held in Delhi made out a case for the 'right to die' by citing evidence that religion permits a person to end his life once the four objectives of life, namely (i) *Dharma* (religion and moral virtues), (ii) *Artha* (wealth), (iii) *Kama* (Love and desire) and (iv) *Moksha* (spiritual enjoyment) have been achieved. Pope John Paul II is also quoted as making the observation: "When inevitably death is imminent in spite of the means used, it is permitted in conscience to take decision to refuse forms of treatment that would only secure precarious and burdensome prolongation of life, so long as the normal care due to a sick person in similar cases is not interrupted..."

It should be clear from the above that the qualifying preconditions laid down in each case make it distinctly different from suicide. Religion, as quoted by G.P. Tripathi, permits one to end his life only after he has achieved the four objectives of life i.e., after one has lived a full, qualitatively rich and meaningful life, which would often be at the attainment of ripe old age, whereas a majority of suicides attempted or committed are by persons in the 18–30 age bracket. Further, this part of religion, barring some rarest of rare exceptions, such as that of Acharya Vinobha Bhave, has become obsolete and dead to all intents and purposes as far as the Hindu masses are concerned. Pope John Paul II makes it crystal clear that only that person who is close to death and it is impossible to stall death by any medical means can refuse to have treatment. It is not even the case of a person suffering from a terminal illness alone but one whose death is imminent. Even if some kind of relevance can be seen in these cases and suicides, it may be argued that it can be termed as a remote or far-fetched relevance. These instances are perhaps more relevant to the issue of the 'right to die'.

The moral aspect also needs to be viewed in its broader perspective. It cannot be kept confined in its application only to the person who commits or attempts to commit suicide. Does the act of suicide not harm, hurt or affect the surviving members of the family? Is not the act of committing suicide by one member of the family a trauma for the other members of the family, the relatives and friends of the deceased person? Does the family, the near and dear ones of the person who commits suicide not suffer emotionally and mentally? A physical injury does harm but an emotional injury and a mental shock harm and hurt even more as the wound caused by these is deeper and hard to heal. It is a completely shattering experience for the entire family. Do the surviving members of the family not suffer the ignominy, social disgrace and shame because the act of suicide still has a social stigma attached to it? And what happens when the person ending his life also happens to be the sole bread winner of the family? Does he not leave them in the lurch? Does he not by overreacting to a situation and by his irrational act seal the fate of those who were dependent on him for their subsistence? Suicide or an attempt to commit suicide is not without its fallout. As a matter of fact a suicide sends a shock wave through the entire neighbourhood. It might even incite other suicide prone persons in the neighbourhood to attempt taking the fatal step. It might even trigger a chain reaction as it did during the anti-Mandal agitation. So it is difficult to say that suicide is not immoral or that it does not harm others. As Shneidmen has observed, "The person who commits suicide puts his psychological skeleton in the survivor's emotional closet."

The apex Court has also made a reference to the practice of *Jauhars* and *Sati*. These practices form a category apart. These can be termed as custom-compelled, primitive, sacrificial acts committed willingly in some cases and in most cases committed unwillingly under compulsion. These cannot be covered under the blanket term 'suicide'. Anyway, the practice of *Sati* is now a criminal offence.

But as a natural corollary to the striking down of Section 309 I.P.C., the question of the 'right to die' may now come into sharp focus and a legal battle may begin for it with a renewed vigour. Significantly, B.N. Colabawalla, Chairman of the Society for the Right to Die With Dignity, in an article published in the *Times of India* of June 12, 1994 hailed the Supreme Court verdict as "a landmark of jurisprudence in the country" and then went on to add: "It has to be hailed as a triumph of rational humanism over outdated legality. Undoubtedly the judgement will raise many debates; and includes in these will be the burning issue of the 'right to die with dignity' and voluntary euthanasia."

The apex Court has, however, observed that "We do not propose to refer to the thinking on this subject (of euthanasia), principally because the same is beyond the scope of the present petitions and also because in euthanasia a third person is either actively or passively involved about whom it may be said that he aids or abets the killing of another person. We propose to make distinction between an attempt of a person to take his life and action of some others to bring to an end the life of a third person. Such a distinction can be made on principle and is conceptually permissible."

But the Court then goes on to add that "...it is nonetheless required to be stated that euthanasia is not much unrelated to the act of suicide inasmuch as wherever passive euthanasia has been held to be permissible under the law one of the requirements insisted is consent of the patient or of his relatives in case the patient be not in a position to give voluntary consent." But the debate will not end here. It shall, in fact, begin from here. The right to die is, after all, "assisted suicide".

The Supreme Court verdict on suicide is a landmark in the history of jurisprudence. It is a progressive judgement which will serve the cause of humanisation of law. And as the Court has observed, "... by effacing Section 309, we would be attuning this part of our criminal law to the global wavelength."

After stating the socio-legal and judicial objectives the apex Court has sought to achieve through this verdict, it goes on to conclude, "Whether we have succeeded or not; and if so, to what extent is for others to judge."

It is doubtless a progressive and humane judgement but it is difficult to say whether it can solve the problem of suicide or make it easy in any way for the survivors of the family of the deceased person to bear the loss. It may be said in conclusion, that while it closes one question, it opens many more. But this perhaps is the true genre of every progressive step.

END NOTES

1. 1985 Cri. L.J. 931.
2. 1987 Cri. L.J. 743.
3. 1988 Cri. L.J. 543.
4. J.T. (Judgements Today) 1994 (3) SC 392.
5. *Id* at p. 422.

Life is a voyage. The winds of life
come strong
From every point; yet each will speed
thy course along,
It thou with steady hand
when tempests blow
Can't keep thy course aright
and never once let go.

Theodore Williams, The Voyage of Life

Chapter 6

DECRIMINALISING SUICIDE

*Nandan Dasgupta**

IN DECLARING Section 309 of the Indian Penal Code to be violative of our Constitution, the highest Court[1] has at last removed an acute embarrassment and disgrace to our culture and society. It is important to remember that it does not do us proud that a law borrowed from a jurisprudence entirely foreign to our culture is being removed from our statute books decades after the correction had been made in the land of its origin. More importantly, the Court has boldly brought into open and discussed at some length in its judgement the need for therapy for such persons. It is now widely believed that so called criminals are merely deviants who have a problem of the psyche and are more in need of sympathy, support and treatment than punishment. Predictably, the Court was not so progressive as that and was quick to distinguish between "psychiatric problems" and "criminal instinct". Yet, what is heartening is that a begining has been made and we may be on the threshold of a debate at the appropriate levels and for a reconsideration of other absurdities (adultery, for example) and also on the need to take an entirely fresh look at our penology.

It is sad, however, that in such a landmark judgement, although recognising that suicide is unnatural behaviour, the Court went on to hold in contradiction on the face of it that it is devoid of adverse sociological effects and that it is not

* Advocate

opposed either to morality or religion. This is most distressing coming as it does from an august office recognised by the populace as one which has been preserving and protecting for them all that is good and precious in life. This is more so as the Court recognises, albeit without making judicial comment, that it is possible that "narcotic addiction, chronic alcoholism, heavy cigarette smoking, reckless driving, other risk taking behaviours" may amount to suicidal behaviour.

Self-preservation is acknowledged as the strongest and the most basic and essential of all animal instincts—that survival instinct which makes the new born babe suckle at its mother's breast without any training. This is an instinct which has been provided by nature not merely for the survival of the individual but in turn also for the preservation of the species. As Dr. Desmond Morris tells us in "The Naked Ape", those animals which have the fiercest weaponry of injury and death exercise the maximum restraint during confrontations within the species in order to prevent annihilation of the species. As usual, it is the wisest of all animals which most often refuses to conform to this amongst other laws of nature. For that matter, other than the unexplained behaviour of lemmings and perhaps other rare incidents, it is only man in the whole of the animal kingdom which resorts so often to self-destruction, violating the protection so thoughtfully implanted in it by nature. Here it may be noted that even the mass suicide of lemmings is a phenomenon so that others may survive and in fact amounts to an act of kindness. Society can never condone destruction, whether it be of others or of self, except by the rule of law, as it will be opposed to the very existence of society. It is interesting to see what John Locke,[2] an English academician and philosopher of the 17th century has to say in this respect:

> But though this be a state of liberty, yet it is not a state of licence; though man in that state have an uncontrollable liberty to dispose of his person or possessions, yet he has no liberty to destroy himself, or so much as any creature in his possession, but where some nobler use than its bare preservation calls for it. The state of Nature has a law of Nature to govern it,

> which obliges everyone, and reason, which is that law, teaches all mankind who will but consult it, that being all equal and independent, no one ought to harm another in his life, health, liberty or possessions; for men being all the workmanship of one omnipotent and infinitely wise Maker; all the servants of one sovereign Master, sent into the world by His order and about His business; they are His property, whose workmanship they are made to last during His, not one another's pleasure. And, being furnished with like faculties, sharing all in one community of Nature, there cannot be supposed any such subordination among us that may authorise us to destroy one another, as if we were made for one another's uses, as the inferior ranks of creatures are for ours. Everyone as he is bound to preserve himself, and not to quit his station wilfully, so by the like reason, when his own preservation comes not in competition, ought he as much as he can to preserve the rest of mankind, and not unless it be to do justice on an offender, take away or impair the life, or what tends to the preservation of the life, the liberty, health, limb, or goods of another.

There are many rules of behaviour that make for peaceful co-existence and maintaining the fragile balance in society which is admittedly more important today than ever before. As a cog in the social machine, every individual owes a debt and a responsibility to his family, his society, his history and culture and also to humanity and to conform to a pattern of socially acceptable and sustainable behaviour. As Kant[3] expresses so lucidly:

> On the other hand, it is a duty to maintain one's life; and, in addition, everyone has also a direct inclination to do so. But on this account the often anxious care which most men take for it has no intrinsic worth, and their maxim has no moral import. They preserve their life as duty requires, no doubt, but not because duty requires. On the other hand, if adversity and

hopeless sorrow have completely taken away the relish for life; if the unfortunate one, strong in mind, indignant at his fate rather than desponding or dejected, wishes for death, and yet preserves his life without loving it—not from inclination or fear, but from duty—then his maxim has a moral worth.

A man reduced to despair by a series of misfortunes feels wearied of life, but is still so far in possession of his reason that he can ask himself whether it would not be contrary to his own life. Now he inquires whether the maxim of his action could become a universal law of nature. His maxim is: "From self-love I adopt it as a principle to shorten my life when its longer duration is likely to bring more evil than satisfaction". It is asked then simply whether this principle founded on self-love can become a universal law of nature. Now we see at once that a system of nature of which it should be a law to destroy life by means of the very feeling whose special nature it is to impel to the improvement of life would contradict itself and, therefore, could not exist as a system of nature; hence that maxim cannot possibly exist as a universal law of nature and, consequently, would be wholly inconsistent with the supreme principle of all duty.

Socrates[4] told his judges:

"If you say to me now that we will acquit you on the condition that you no longer discourse in the way you have hitherto discoursed, nor trouble either our young or our old men," I shall answer, "You make yourselves ridiculous by thinking that, if one of our commanders had appointed me to a captain post, it is my duty to keep and maintain it, and to resolve to die a thousand times rather than desert it; but if God has put us in any place and way of life, we ought to desert it."

All the great civilisations and religions have recognised this need for restrained behaviour and have criticised and censured in some form or other self-destruction as not only being unnatural and irresponsible but also detrimental in general to maintaining social balance. The only great civilisation—the Roman—which glorified suicide has perished.

Plato[5] is said to have spoken with contempt in his *Laws* of him who resorts to suicide led by cowardice and not by disgrace, accident of fortune or public judgement. One is inclined to disagree with him now inasmuch as suicide for any ostensible reason would in today's context be wholly insupportable as being an act of aggression against society. Our society today is wallowing in the dregs of morality and individual character is at rock bottom. Reaffirmation of values is the crying need of the hour.

Whether or not suicide requires or deserves penal deterrence could be a matter of debate (now set at rest by the Court) but there can be no doubt that it cannot be afforded social condonation or glorification. On the question of the right to commit suicide, Hegel[6] state:

> A single person, I need hardly say, is something subordinate, and as such he must dedicate himself to the ethical whole. Hence if the state claims life, the individual must surrender it. But may a man take his own life? Suicide may at a first glance be regarded as act of courage, but only the false courage of tailors and servant girls. Or again it may be looked upon as a misfortune, since it is inward distraction which leads to it. But the fundamental question is: Have I a right to take my life? The answer will be that I, as this individual, am not master of my life, because life, as the comprehensive sum of my activity, is nothing external to personality, which itself is this immediate personality. Thus when a person is said to have a right over his life, the words are a contradiction, because they mean that a person has a right over himself. But he has no such right, since he does not stand over himself and he cannot pass judgement on himself. When Hercules destroyed himself by fire and when

Brutus fell on his sword, this was the conduct of a hero against his personality. But as for an unqualified right to suicide, we must simply say that there is no such thing, even for heros.

The various causes leading to suicide would usually be either fear of pain, physical or otherwise, or fear of a fate worse than death. "A fate worse than death" would include the so-called fear of disgrace in those high school children who fail to live up to their own or to their parent's expectations in examinations and those romantics whose advances of passion have been spurned. It is frightening to think that such wayward behaviour is entitled to social sanction by comparison with the "fasting unto death" political threats of Mahatma Gandhi (para 81) or the death obtained through "*Samadhi*". In fact, it is peculiar that *Samadhi* should at all be thought to be suicide—then perhaps taking of *sanyas* may also be called desertion. "Fate worse than death" would also cover the fear of assault on the chastity of a woman. Yet we have outlawed the practice of "*Sati*" which had found its roots in this fear. The practice was no doubt outlawed at a time when social circumstances had changed, the fear no longer existed and the practice had by then found other reasons and vested interests. In fact, what was outlawed was by then not suicide but murder. Would this then historically show that social acceptance of any form of suicide may eventually lead to condonation of murder? Is it not correct that at one point of time "*Sati*" was not just voluntary but even honourable (one is reminded of "Hara-kiri") but an act which gradually became a cruel ritual and a blot on society? Should we then not refuse to condone the act of suicide for any reason whatever as being too fraught with the danger of not remaining an aberration to but becoming a part of the social fabric one day to become a Frankenstein and to tear it asunder?

It is no doubt easy for one to preach patience to another not having himself ever gone through deprivation or ignominy to such a degree where reason is overtaken by desperation. Yet it is necessary to say that even if everyone is not strong enough to fight the war called life, it is not fair for anyone to decide upon the point of time where he can say,

"I give up". After all, history is full of examples of those who gave up too soon and those who lived on to succeed. Human circumstances are strange and circumstances have an even stranger way of changing and it is only the foolish or conceited that can say that they can predict the future. To quote more fully the poet Henley[7] cited by the Court in the begining of its judgement:

Out of the night that covers me,
black as the pit from pole to pole,
I thank whatever gods may be,
For my unconquerable soul.

In the fell clutch of circumstance,
I have not winced nor cried aloud:
Under the bludgeonings of chance
My head is bloody, but unbowed.

Beyond this place of wrath and tears
Looms but the horror of the shade,
And yet the menace of the years,
Finds and shall find me unafraid.

It matters not how strait the gate,
How charged with punishments the scroll,
I am the master of my fate,
I am the captain of my soul.

This writer feels that since the Court could have come to the conclusion that Section 309 of the Penal Code violated Article 21 our Constitution without having to proclaim that the act was not against morality and religion, it should not have done so. In the passing, it should be noted that with distressing regularity the Court has been treading on areas which more appropriately need to be and have been historically solved on the streets, on the warfields and at the ballot boxes rather than in Court rooms. Having repeatedly set the limits for the Legislature, the Executive and the subordinate Judiciary, the Court now needs to set certain parameters for itself too. It should be able to say, "this is a matter where we can interfere but we will not". Perhaps Babri Masjid is a recent case in point. Anyhow, the Court should hardly take on any mantle other than judicial and refrain from explaining to us what is religion and how suicide is quite in conformity with religion. Taking up the logic of the Court, perhaps even murder is not against religion for as the Court tells us in one paragraph, "Life does not end in this world" and "one who takes life may not really be taken to have put an end to his whole life". The Court, while probably referring to death as a result of *Samadhi*, says in paragraph 33 that "this desire for communion with God may very rightly lead even a very healthy mind to think that he would forego his right to live and would rather choose not to live". While entirely agreeing with this comment as also the basic finding of the Court, this writer is unable to agree with the Court that suicide is neither immoral nor against religion and again wonders whether it was really necessary for the Court to be a commentator on morality and religion?

END NOTES

1. *P. Rathinam/Nagabhusan Patnaik v. Union of India* J.T. 1994 (3) SC 392.
2. *An Essay Concerning the True Original Extent and End of Civil Government, Chapter II,* John Locke (1632–1704).
3. *Fundamental Principles of the Metaphysic of Morals, First Section*, Immanuel Kant by Thomas Kingsmill Abbott.
4. *Discourses*, Book I, Epictetus (60–138) as translated by George Long; Plato Apology, as translated by Benjamin Jowett.
5. Michel Euquem de Montaigne (1533–1592). The Essays, as translated by Charles Cotton; Plato Laws, Book IX.
6. George Wilhelm Friedrich Hegel (1770–1831) Philosophy of Right as translated by T.M. Knox.
7. William Ernest Henley (1849–1903). Out of the Night.

Chapter 7

A SUICIDAL VERDICT ON SUICIDE

*Krishan Mahajan**

THE RIGHT to kill oneself by one's own hand has been upheld by the Supreme Court as the correlated negative aspect of the fundamental right to life under Article 21 of the Constitution. This has been done in the course of a judgement declaring that Section 309 Indian Penal Code which makes attempt to commit suicide (or an unsuccessful suicide) into a criminal offence, is unconstitutional as it is violative of Article 21.

The April 26, 1994 judgement by Justices R.M. Sahai and B.L. Hansaria in *P. Rathinam* v. *UOI* [1] carries inherent contradictions. The first is that while holding Section 309 I.P.C. as unconstitutional the judgement nowhere states whether the section violates the right to life in Article 21 or the newly declared right to die. Every survivor of an unsuccessful suicide therefore is a person whose right to die has been infringed by those who saved him and made his bid unsuccessful. To use the language of the judgement, all those who saved the person committing suicide "forced him to enjoy the right to life to his detriment, disadvantage or disliking". In terms of legal logic such a person should have a remedy in the courts for infringement of his right to die. What relief will the courts give him—an order to ensure completion of his suicide or to be compensated by all those who saved him? In terms of its own distinction between abet-

* Advocate, Supreme Court and Legal Columnist.

ting suicide and committing suicide the court cannot give the order for completion of suicide since then it would be abetting it. The same distinction prohibits the court from a compensation order since the court itself has stated that abetment of suicide is a valid offence. The other problem before the court would be one of waiver of fundamental rights. Under current law none can waive their fundamental rights even though illiteracy and poverty practically amount to a waiver. But assuming, a necessary assumption to make the court's right to die workable, that one can waive a fundamental right, which one can be considered to have been waived? Is it that a survivor of a suicide bid can be said to have waived his right to life to claim the right to die and on being unsuccessful has an option again?

By virtue of the judgement's right to die the option to die again would be available. But then the necessary and incidental measures necessary to effectuate the fundamental right to die must be accessible. However, anyone making such access possible—poison, instruments, ropes, rooms—is liable to be punished for abetment of suicide.

The basis of the judgement for declaring a fundamental right to die is based on its answer to one of its questions—"Does commission of suicide damage the monopolistic power of the state to take life?" The court answers that "nobody can claim to have monopoly over a human life. It is God alone who can claim such a power. If a person takes his life, he is taking his own life, and not the life of anybody else; and so, the argument that State's monopolistic power of taking life is taken away by the person who attempts to commit suicide has no legs to stand."[2]

This philosophical basis of the judgement is highly debatable and questionable. The State as a symbol of organised community life is bound in law to invest in its people to enable them to participate in such life and then participate on a basis of equality. When the life of an individual is knitted into a community through legal institutions of taxation and people's representatives, can it still be said that in an attempted suicide a person is taking his own life only?

Further a State uses its constitutional and legal machinery in a manner to create a socio-economic structure that kills the desire to live in the majority of its citizens. In short, it throws Directive Principles overboard and in flagrant violation of its own laws, including the Constitution, women and children are victimised. The judgement enables State victims of unconstitutional economics to liberate the State by killing themselves. The tragedy is that this judicial euthanasia is given for the majority of Indians by an eight line philosophy by declaring that in suicide a person takes his own life only and stating that the issue of state monopoly over human bodies is "not a point required to be gone into detail". Is it surprising that economically condemned Indians never enabled, and disabled by the State from the national economy having thereby no capacity to enjoy the various constitutional freedoms of the living are given by the apex court the fundamental right of physical self-liquidation? This is the logical result of a court refusing to apply public interest and human rights principles in revenue cases and not devising any machinery for effective follow-up of its public interest litigation judgements. It is also the logical result of a concept of territorial jurisdiction of courts as power without any accountability about its non-use for legal care of the people in that jurisdiction. If each person owns his body then each body is left to its own remedies howsoever unequal these may be.

All this arises because the judgement chose to widen the area of debate by formulating 16 questions, many of which the apex court has often refused on the ground of these being in the realm of policy. The judgement even arranges these questions in order of comparative importance and the question concerning the philosophy of the verdict finds a place at the tail end.

There was a need to say how far medical knowledge and treatment had advanced to treat suicides. There was a need to address oneself to the specific issue of suicides in a developing economy and the sociology of suicides. All this was necessary to conclude that criminalisation of the attempt to commit suicide had become unreasonable, unfair and unjust. The basis for this would have remained the fundamental right to life with life marching in pace with current knowledge. This would have required the fastening of a liability on the State for the medical treatment of suicide. That did not happen as the debate was unnecessarily and needlessly pushed to the right to die which left even the judges in an uncomfortable quandary of trying to distinguish between suicide and passive euthanasia even while denying that they were dealing with the issue of mercy killing. People of India unite—you have nothing to lose but life!

END NOTES

1. AIR 1994, SC 1844.
2. *Id.* at 1866.

Chapter 8

CAN WE DIE AS A MATTER OF RIGHT

*P.S. Lathwal**

RIGHT TO life is most fundamental of all other rights. Various thinkers have given their opinion on this issue. Rousseau expressed that every one has a right to even risk his life in order to protect it. Locke states that one cannot take away one's own life and cannot also permit to deprive him of it.[1] Thomas Hobbes also emphasized upon this view.[2]

Taking one's own life intentionally and voluntarily i.e. suicide, was objected to by Plato and Aristotle on the ground that state loses a citizen. Kant stressed that man's freedom may be employed to enable him to live as a man but he can not use his freedom to destroy himself.[3]

In India Section 309 of the Indian Penal Code, 1860 makes, an attempt to suicide, an offence punishable with simple imprisonment of one year or with fine or both. Our judiciary has had occasion to deal with this aspect many times.

In *C. Jagadeeswar* v. *State of Andhra Pradesh*,[4] the Bench upheld the Constitutional validity of Section 309 of I.P.C., 1860. The court observed:

> Unless a man is assured of physical existence, there can be no fundamental right. Since the state exists for the common good of the citizens, no Constitution can ignore the rights of the citizens to life though it may not be explicity explained. In these circumstances,

* Lecturer in Law, M.D. University, Rohtak.

> it is rather difficult to hold that the right to life impliedly guaranteed by the constitution of India, includes the right to die.

The Court went further:

> To confer a right to destroy oneself and to take it away from the perview of the Courts to enquire into the act would be one step down in the scene of human distress and motivation.

The then Chief Justice Sachar of Delhi High Court in *State* v. *Sanjay Kumar*,[5] observed, "the continuance of Section 309 of I.P.C. is an anachronism unworthy of human society like ours. Medical clinics for such social misfits certainly, but police and prison never". On this ground the Court upheld the acquittal of a young boy under Section 309 of the Penal Code.

Also in *Maruti Shripati Dubal* v. *State of Maharashtra*,[6] the Bombay High Court, declaring Section 309 of I.P.C. unconstitutional as violative of Article 14 and 21, held that right to live, guaranteed under Art. 21 of the Constitution, includes also a right to die[7] and the impugned section violated it in so far as it made suicide an offence. Desire to die, according to judges, is not unnatural but abnormal and uncommon.

Thus the question arises, does one have a right to commit suicide? Is this right a part of personal liberty protected under Article 21? Is it the same thing as right to die with dignity? Is it distinguishable from euthanasia? What is the position in different countries in this regard? The Bombay High Court in *Dubal* case listed diseases, cruel or unbearable condition of life (mental or physical), a sense of shame or disenchantment with life—may be physical disability in war or battle, as several circumstances in which people may wish to end their lives. It holds that every one should have the freedom to dispose of his life as and when he desires.[8]

The poor and weak may opt for suicide, some depression or humiliation may prompt some to take this extreme step.

Although this liberal approach of the Bombay High Court on suicide may help many but is sure to give rise to certain issues, like:

i. Some women may be pressurized to commit the barbaric and inhuman act of '*sati*'.[9] Since in traditional societies individual decision matters little.
ii. In cases where people go on hunger strike, the police will be unable to arrest and prosecute them.
iii. Suicide owing to frustration in love, examination or failure to get a job or promotion in service may raise many social problems.

In cases of threatened self-immolation or other potentially explosive situation, the police would not be able to take action. Incidental death may invite different problems.

Does individual have no responsibility/accountability of his life towards State when he claims that it is the constitutional duty of the State to protect his life and liberty. Can it be destroyed at his own level as and when he desires? Right to life may not imply right to death. The aims and objectives of Article 21 are to protect life and personal liberty. Hence, the right to die or to interfere with his own life will totally defeat these aims and objectives. Article 21 is preserving and protecting life and personal liberty and, therefore, no contrary interpretation is acceptable. In simple words right to die or the right to take one's life are distortion and antithetic concepts of Article 21, and, therefore, not tenable.

In *Maruti Shripati Dubal*, the failure of the State to provide a means of livelihood and thereby an access to life may in terms of natural justice create an exception for a person to end his life. But is it not our duty in civilized society to work and fight these conditions which defeat life itself? Can rendering a section ultra-vires solve the problem and stop the work of civilized society?

In the present competitive world, frustration and/or depression have become part and parcel of life. These drift individual towards committing suicide. Daughter-in-law and elderly invalids in families could be coerced into committing suicide. Dowry deaths passing off as suicides are at high rates. In absence of Section 309 of I.P.C. there may be minimum scope for intervention of law and inquiry into such cases.

Thus in view of the judgement, of the Andhra High Court, attempt to suicide is an offence whereas the Delhi and Bombay High Court held, it to be, a right to die. It is a very important matter to be discussed in the present context of society where people lack in the basic/bare necessities of food, clothing, shelter, medical facilities and education and where circumstances compel some people to sell or pledge their off spring for money and sell their blood or organs for livelihood.

In the recent historic judgement, in *P. Rathinam/ Nagabhusan Patnaik* v. *Union of India*[10] the Supreme Court has declared as unconstitutional and hence void Section 309 of the Indian Penal Code which makes "attempt to suicide" a punitive offence. While making the declaration the judges also quashed criminal proceedings initiated against Nagbhushan Patnaik in the Court of Sub-judge at Gunpur in Koraput district of Orissa for attempt to suicide.

Taking into consideration the views of the high court of Delhi, Bombay and Andhra Pradesh on the issue the Judges held:

> Section 309 of the Indian Penal Code deserves to be effaced from the statute book to humanise our penal laws. It is cruel and irrational provision and it may result in punishing a person again (doubly), who has suffered agony and would be under going ignominy (which is definitely a punishment though not a corporal one) because of his failure to commit suicide.[11]

The Judges made it clear that the act of suicide could not be said to be against religion, morality or public policy and an act of attempted suicide has no baneful effect on society. Further, suicide or attempt to suicide causes no harm to others, because of which the state's interference with the personal liberty of the concerned person is not called for.

The Court, therefore, held that Section 309 violated Article 21 of our Constitution and so, it was void. It remarked:

> May it be said that the view taken by us would advance not only the cause of humanisation, which is a need of the day, but of globalisation also, as by effacting Section 309, we would be attuning this part of criminal law to global wave length," the Judges commented.[12]

It may be noted here that attempted suicide was removed from the penal laws of U.K. in 1961 and is not an offence in the U.S.A. and U.S.S.R.

As early as in 1971, our law commission took up this issue and recommended that the penal provision of Section 309 of Indian Penal Code, being harsh and unjustified, should be replaced.[13] An Amendment Bill (to the I.P.C.) was introduced in Rajya Sabha seeking to delete Section 309. Rajya Sabha passed it in November, 1978. The Bill however lapsed and could not get through since the Lok Sabha was dissolved in 1979 while it was pending.

The Supreme Court quoted Mahatma Gandhi who once observed, "death is our friend, the truest of friends. He delivers us from agony. I do not want to die of a creeping paralysis of my faculties—a defeated man". The Court also quoted the English Poet William Ernest Henloy, "I am the master of my fate, I am Captain of my soul" and observed, "if the decision to die is implemented to its fructification resulting in death that is the end of the matter, the dead is relieved of the agony, the pain and suffering and no evil consequences known to our law follow. But if the person concerned be unfortunate to survive, the attempt to commit suicide may see him behind the bars, as the same is punishable under Section 309 of the Indian Penal Code.

> In any case a person can not be forced to enjoy his right to life to his deteriment, disadvantage or disliking. As in case of a women who attempted suicide after being raped, it will "add insult to injury", if she was made to face trial for an unsuccessful suicide attempt.[14]

The right to live (under Article 21) can be said to include the right not to live a forced life. If a law was cruel it would be violative of Article 21 and punishment for attempted suicide needed psychiatric treatment (for better understanding, counselling or therapeutic intervention) instead of being treated as criminal, the court noted.

Regarding euthanasia, the Court expressed its view that it is not much unrelated to the act of committing suicide in as much as wherever passive euthanasia has been held to be permissible under the law, one of the requirements is the consent of the patient or of his relation in case the patient be not in a position to give voluntary consent. In euthanasia or mercy killing, according to the court a third person was either actively or passively involved, aiding or abetting the killing of another person. Persons aiding or abetting suicide were on different footing and covered by another law.[15]

Section 306 of the Indian Penal Court says, those abetting suicide could be punished with imprisonment upto 10 years. Now when suicide is no offence, how can its abetment be an offence? People who actively assist suicide will go scot free.

The decision sounds path-breaking and historic, but there are reservations. The fairly long judgement explains that Section 309 has been used in inhumane manner as in unsuccessful attempt at suicide, the individual is fated to lead a forced life. Basing its view on it, the Court concluded that 'suicide' has no baneful effect on society and thus "state intervention with personal liberty of the concerned is not called for". The next obvious step in this line of thinking is to refer to the "social dynamics of criminal law" and "functional theory of sentencing and therapeutic reach of punitive acts". These are then distilled in a single injunction to "humanise" criminal law and make suicide legal.

Legal and other experts, in a symposium[16] on the issue of 'suicide' felt that this Supreme Court judgement is a right step in order that none should be punished for an attempt to commit suicide.

"The right to live includes the right to die and to penalise a person, who does not want to live, is wrong", maintained P.M. Bakshi the Director of the Indian Law Institute. The judgement, according to him, had given a new direction to Article 21 (the right to life) of the Constitution.

P.P. Rao, Senior Advocate, Supreme Court, felt the proper course for two judges who gave the judgement would have been to refer the issue to a bench of five judges.

It is submitted that if attempt to suicide is to cause or to create public disorder, to defame or to cause mental injury to another or to pressurize for political gains or to compel another to do or not to do an act contrary to law i.e. a step to attract others' attention, then it must certainly invite punishment. But suicide in agony, helplessness and when life is full of grave miseries and result of mental sickness, is justifiable.

For one thing, Section 309 was not so much a punitive provision. It was only to light a moral path, to guide a deeply disturbed, frustrated and depressed mind—away from extreme action. The law until now was content to proclaim a social diction—"Live and do not die"—and rap the knuckle of those who defied this but lived to obey the rule with profit.[17]

Also, suicide marks the lowest point in a man's incapacity to live, to cope with life, to adjust himself to the demands of life. In that case, he may have no option but to snuff out his life. But the society, of whom he is one of the essential parts, can and must rush to shield him from total loss. If life and liberty are sacrosanct then equally sacrosanct is nursing life and liberty. The society is collective organisation of all men and women. Loss of one man is loss of one limb of society.

John Donne said, "Death be not proud". At the same time, it is necessary to say, "suicide be not proud" because it takes something very precious from the society that can not be replaced.

END NOTES

1. John Locke, *Two Treatise of Government*, P. Lalett (ed.) (New York, 1965) 325 & 402.
2. Hobbes, *Leviathan*, (Penguin Books 1965) 199.
3. Parikh, S.N., "Rights to Life and Unborn Person", *Indian Bar Volume* 11(3), (1984) p. 287. See also Kant, *Lecture on Ethics* (New York, 1963) 119.
4. 1983 Cri. L.J. 549.
5. 1985 Cri. L.J. 931.

6. 1987 Cri. L.J. 743.
7. See R. Hazare, "Punishing attempted Suicide Challenged" *Lawyers Collective* (August, 1986) p. 14. Lalita Iyer, "Suicide—Right to End one's life", *Lex ET Juris* - the Law Magazine (Sept. 1986) 36. V.S. Despande —"To be or not to be". (1984) *3 SCC.* (Journal Section) p. 10. G.S. Tewari—"The Plea for Right Not to Live vis-a-vis the Indian Constitution", *AIR 1986* (Journal Section) 38.
8. See S.P. Sathe, "Constitutional Law-1"—*A.S.I.L.* XXII (1986) 359 at 388.
9. *All India Democratic Women's Association and Janwad Samiti v. Union of India.* AIR 1989 SC 1280 (wherein the validity of the Commission of *Sati* (Prevention) Act 1987 was challenged).
10. AIR 1994 SC 1844.
11. *Id.* at 1868.
12. *Ibid.*
13. Law Commission of India 42 Report 1971, paragraph 16.33.
14. See Ajay Ahuja, "Attempted Suicide—Not a matter of life and death", *The Tribune*, Chandigarh, May 14, 1994, p. 4.
15. See "Supreme Court Strikes down Punishment for attempted suicide" *The Times of India*, New Delhi, April 28, 1994, p. 1.
16. "Order on Suicide hailed", in a discussion organised by The Indian Law Institute and United Lawyers Association—reported in *Times of India*, July 17, 1994.
17. See *The Tribune*, Chandigarh, April 29, 1994, See also: Raine M.L. "Literacy echo of Suicide Verdict", *The Tribune*, May 2, 1994, Rajinder Singh, "Supreme Court Verdict—A Cause to Rejoice"? *The Tribune*, May 14, 1994.

Chapter 9

RIGHT TO SUICIDE

*Kusum**

"You ever gentle gods, take my breath from me;
Let not my worser spirit tempt me again
To die before you please."

Shakespeare: "King Lear"

SUICIDE—THE act of voluntary and intentional self-destruction, has been viewed with instinctive horror and revulsion in some societies, whereas in others, it has been extolled. According to the Koran, suicide is a crime more heinous and grave than homicide. Plato condemned it: "They must have no companions whatsoever in the tomb, for they must be buried ignominously in waste and nameless spots. . . and the tomb be marked with neither headstone nor name." Plato, however, exempted from such censure those who took their own lives through intolerable stress or because of a major disgrace. Aristotle condemned suicide as an act of cowardice. Christianity opposed self destruction. According to St. Augustine, suicide was a violation of the commandment. "Thou shalt not kill"—a commandment which applied to all innocent lives, one's own and others'. According to St. Thomas Acquinas, God alone had control over life and death and one who decides the moment of his death, commits or attempts suicide, usurps Gods' power.

* Associate Research Professor, Indian Law Institute, New Delhi.

Some civilisations and societies, on the other hand, honoured suicide. In India, for example, the *Brahmins* honoured the person who "voluntarily freed his body." A widow who died on the pyre of her husband and committed *sati*, was extolled. The Greeks permitted criminals who were convicted of certain offences to put an end to their lives. Drinking the hemlock by Socrates is another example.

Today, many countries have abolished attempt to commit suicide as a crime. Abetment or inducement to commit suicide, however, is a crime every where. Under the English law prior to 1961, attempted suicide was a misdemeanour punishable with fine or imprisonment. There were strong opinions against it. According to one English writer:[1]

> It seems a monstrous procedure to inflict further suffering on even a single individual who has already found life so unbearable, his chances of happiness so slender, that he has been willing to face pain and death in order to cease living. That those for whom life is altogether bitter should be subjected to further bitterness and degradation seems perverse legislation.

Under the Suicide Act, 1961, attempt to commit suicide is no longer a crime under the English law. In the United States and U.S.S.R. attempted suicide is not a crime. Even in Japan where the custom of compulsory Seppuku (hara-kiri) or ritual of embowelling as a mode of punishment was made illegal in 1868, voluntary hara-kiri and an act of self-defeat or self-sacrifice has always been highly praised. In India, Section 309 of the Indian Penal Code penalises an attempt to commit suicide with imprisonment for a term which may extend to one year or with fine, or with both. It is pertinent to note that under the original sections, prior to 1882, a sentence of imprisonment however short, was compulsory. Now the court has discretion and may just impose a fine.

The serious debate on whether to decriminalise suicide or retain it in the penal code has at last been put an end to—at least legally, and perhaps only legally, by the Supreme Court judgement in *P. Rathinam, Nagabhushan Patnaik* v. *Union of India*[2]. The history of this case is as follows:

As early as 1971 the Law Commission took up this issue and recommended that the penal provision of Section 309 is harsh and unjustified and so should be repealed. In 1979 a Bill was introduced in the Rajya Sabha seeking to delete Section 309 but it lapsed on the dissolution of the Lok Sabha soon after. In 1984, Justice Sachar (the then Chief Justice of the Delhi High Court) collectively quashed 119 cases of attempted suicide pending in the criminal courts and directed the administration and the police not to prosecute such victims in future. In 1985, the same judge upheld the acquittal of an accused charged under Section 309.[3] He observed: "It is ironic that Section 309 I.P.C. still continues to be on our Penal Code. The result is that a young boy driven to such frustration so as to escape one's own life would have escaped human punishment if he had succeeded but is to be hounded by the police, because attempt was foiled. Strange paradox that in the age of votaries of euthanasia, suicide should be criminally punishable .... The continuance of Section 309 I.P.C. is an anachronism unworthy of human society like ours. Medical clinics for such social misfits certainly, but police and prisons, never." In *Maruti Shripati* v. *State of Maharashtra*[4] the provision was challenged as being violative of Article 21 of the Constitution. A police constable was facing prosecution for attempting to immolate himself outside the commissioner's office. The court accepted the petition filed by his wife challenging the constitutional validity of Section 309. It observed, "There is nothing unnatural about the desire to die and hence with the right to die whatever the circumstances which induce a person to end or terminate his life; the act of termination of life is the act of that individual. It is no less his than his act of living."

It was held that under Article 21, the right to life includes the right not to live or not to be forced to live. So far as the deterrent value of punishment in these cases is concerned, the court held that in case of persons with mental disorders, what is needed is psychiatric treatment and not confinement in prison cells which is going to make their condition worse. Those attempting suicide on account of acute physical ailment etc., need nursing homes and not prisons to prevent them from making the attempts again. In case of those who want to die for social or political cause or because of loss of interest in life, no deterrence can hold them back from attempting again. The Andhra Pradesh High Court however, took a different stand in a case before it, in 1987.[5] The appellant, who was a doctor, had killed his four minor children by administering some poisonous tablets and later attempted to commit suicide alongwith his wife. The session court convicted him for murder and for attempted suicide. In appeal, the Andhra Pradesh High Court observed "unless a man is assured of physical existence there can be no other fundamental right." And further, "if attempt to commit suicide is not an offence, people who actually assist and induce persons to commit suicide may go scot free."

The constitutional validity of Section 309 was accordingly, upheld. Writ petitions were filed before the Supreme Court on the issue of validity or otherwise of Section 309. The prosecution of the petitioner who was arrested for going on a hunger strike and was being tried in a court in Orissa, was stayed.

The Supreme Court, by its sensational judgement,[6] has set all doubts and uncertainties at rest by holding against the constitutional validity of Section 309. In a very well researched judgement, the court has discussed the issue on the touchstone of constitutionality, morality, religion, ethics, public policy, secularism, expediency, sociology, humanitarianism, etc. The position in other countries has also been discussed. Holding Section 309 as violative of Article 21, it has held, "Section 309 of the Penal Code deserves to be effaced from the statute book to humanise our penal laws. It is a cruel and irrational provision, and it may result in punishing a person again (doubly) who has suffered agony and would be undergoing ignominy because of his failure to commit suicide. Then, an act of suicide cannot be said to be against religion, morality or public policy, and an act of attempted suicide has no baneful effect on society, further, suicide or attempt to commit it causes no harm to others, because of which states' interference with the personal liberty of the concerned person is not called for." And further said the court.[7]

> . . . . the view taken by us would advance not only the cause of humanisation, which is a need of the day, but of globalisation also, as by effacing Section 309, we would be attuning this part of our criminal law to the global wave length.

This judgement may have come as a hope of liberation to some who are in a very depressed and irreversible state of mind or body, without fear of any punishment should their attempt fail, but what about its effect on young immature minds which tend to act or react in desperate haste? For such people probably the strongest deterrent against the extreme step would have been the penal provision. Some frustrations and depressions in life could be just passing phases like, failure in examination, in love, in getting a job etc. and a person who has no one to give him solace at that particular time might take the extreme step without fear of any law. Also, one wonders the impact of the judgement on dowry killers. Many dowry death cases which could be instigation or abetment to commit suicide by girls could be manoeuvered or interpreted as simple suicide by the girl. Though there are separate laws to deal with such crimes yet the stringency would be considerably diluted. The law needs to be humanised no doubt but it would be dangerous to give a license to everyone to end his/her life irrespective of the situations and circumstances. There should not be a blanket protective shield behind every attempted suicide. Not that a person who takes such a step should be necessarily punished—and that is rarely done in fact—but there must be some force to restrain him from taking the step. Though the fear of a penal law is not the ideal force, yet so long as we do not have adequate services by way of organisations or societies to give solace, counselling and requisite help to the victims of frustration, we need some authority at least to check unbridled acts of attempts to suicide. In any case, all situations cannot be treated alike.

Neither all victims of such attempts should be absolved, nor all such victims deserve to be penally treated. What is needed is a humanising of the *judicial approach* (which in fact is there already) rather than humanising a law by deleting a section without regard to subjectivity.

END NOTES

1. H. Romilly Fedden *Suicide* (1938).
2. 1994 J.T. 1994 (3) SC 392.
3. *State* v. *Sanjay Kumar Bhatia* 1985 Cri. L.J. 931 (Delhi).
4. 1987 Cri. L.J. 743 (Bom.).
5. *C. Jagadeeswar* v. *State of A.P.* 1988 Cr. L.J. 549 (A.P.).
6. *Supra* note 2.
7. *Id.* at p. 423.

Chapter 10

SUICIDE: A PSYCHO-SOCIAL PROBLEM

*S.K. Bhattacharyya**

THE TERM 'suicide' has been variously defined by different scholars. Freud defined suicide as an intra-psychic phenomenon originating primarily within the unconscious as life and death forces are in constant conflict within the individual. Similarly, Gregory Zilboorg viewed suicide as a way of thwarting outside sources which are making life impossible. Karl Menninger describes suicide as the winning of the death instinct over the life instinct under conditions of stress and strain. He further opined that a self-destroyer suffers from (1) the wish to die, (2) the desire to kill, and (3) the desire to be killed. Shneidman defined it as 'the human act of self-inflicted, self-intended cessation'. According to Durkheim, the term 'suicide' is applied to any death which is the direct or indirect result of a positive or negative act accomplished by the victim himself.

The institution of suicide is as old as mankind (Zilboorg). Almost all the ancient civilisations of the world—India, Greek, Latin and others were familiar with it. Greek and Latin civilisations had often seen their best representative men lost to them by means of suicide (Morselli). In fact, the story of suicide is the story of man's various social, economic and religious problems and his relentless struggle against failure to overcome these problems. In India, the history of Vedic age is replete with numerous examples of suicides committed on

* Advocate, Supreme Court of India.

religious grounds. The Mahabharata and the Ramayana are also full of instances of religious suicides. In the days of yore, suicides were also committed on a mass scale. In the Harshacharita, after the death of Prabhakaravardhana, many friends, ministers and servants of the King did away with their lives. Similarly, *Jauhar* was a form of mass suicide prevalent among the Rajputs to avoid intolerable shame. Padmini's embracing fire along with her female attendants with a view to preserving their honour and chastity is a glaring example in this respect. The Atharva-Veda refers to the practice of '*Sati*' through which many women were consigned to flames against their wishes. The latest horrible incident at Deorala in Rajasthan where a young woman was thrown into the funeral pyre of her husband, was glorified by some people in the name of religion. This had, of course, created a lot of furore and indignation all over the country and the people in general rose in revolt against this evil practice. In 1666 A.D., all communities in Russia hailed with enthusiasm, the gospel of death first by starvation, then by famine and finally by fire. Similar was the practice among the early Germans, the Greeks and the Romans and others (Thakur). In Japan, Harakiri is a common type of suicide even now. The famous novelist Kawabata is said to have committed Harakiri. In China also, suicide was common among all classes and persons of all ages. The most common methods of suicide in that country were hanging, leaping down from a wall and opium-poisoning, etc. In the early Hebrew history, suicide is referred to as an escape from the consequences of political and military defeat. In 73 A.D., a number of Jews chose mass suicide in preference to capture and enslavement by the Romans. Among the Jainas, death by fasting as religious suicide was in vogue. However, Buddhism is entirely opposed to the practice of achieving *nirvana* by committing suicide. Kautilya has condemned those who committed suicide under the infatuation of love, anger and other sinful passions. The Brahmapurana holds the views that those who commit suicide by poison, fire, hanging, drowning, falling from a cliff or a tree, should be classed with those who commit great sins. The Vishnu Sanhita also condemns such persons. Inspite of condemnations by ancient religious authorities, suicide has continued to be practised since times immemorial.

Zilboorg observed that "it is clear that the problem of suicide from the scientific point of view remains unsolved. Neither common sense nor clinical psychopathology has found a causal or even a strictly empirical solution." Freud had also made a similar statement while delineating his views on suicide. However, Freud's paper "Mourning and Melancholia" which depicted the dynamics of depression provided the framework for the psychoanalytic theory of suicide. He opined that "the ego sees itself deserted by the super ego and lets itself die." On the other hand, Durkheim approached the problem of suicide from a sociological point of view. He described four types of suicide, viz., (1) egoistic, (2) altruistic, (3) anomic and (4) fatalistic. Egoistic suicide occurs when the individual feels cut off from society. His family links are very weak and he has few friends. Thus, his ties with society and his feeling of belonging to a community are lacking. This feeling of loneliness is a major cause of suicide. Man by nature does not want to live a lonely life. If he is shunned by his relatives and friends and he finds that his aspiration to live with them in the community is frustrated, he may commit suicide. On the contrary, altruistic suicide results from too much integration of the individual into his society and in obedience to the customs of his society he does not hesitate to take his own life. The examples of *Jauhar* in medieval India and Harakiri in Japan may be cited in this connection. The third type of suicide, i.e., anomic suicide is most common in times of social upheaval or economic depression when an individual takes his life not because of physical hardships or poverty but because of the resulting state of anomic and normlessness. He feels that his habitual norms are no longer appropriate to the existing social standards. The fourth type of suicide, i.e., fatalistic suicide, is caused due to oppressive discipline and regulation.

The common methods of attempting or committing suicide in India are: sleeping pills, hanging, drowning, burning, getting run over by automobiles or rains, jumping from heights, etc. As regards causes, suicides are generally committed in the country due to failure in examinations, quarrel with parents-in-law, quarrel with spouse, poverty, love affairs, insanity, dispute over property, dreadful diseases, unemployment, bankruptcy, sudden change of economic position, deaths of dear persons, fall in social reputation, etc. Besides these causes, there is one important factor in our socio-cultural milieu which leads to suicidal deaths. In Indian society marriages are generally arranged by parents within the same caste and solemnised on traditional lines. Personal choice of marital partners against parental wish or forced marriages sometimes lead to suicides. Dowry is also one of the main factors for pathological relationship among the members of the family. Although dowry has been prohibited by law, in actual practice marriages are, in a large number of cases, solemnised on the basis of the quantum of dowry offered by the brides' parents. In the case of insufficient dowry received by the bridegroom at the time of marriage, his parents become displeased and their ire falls on the bride and she becomes a victim of torture in the hands of her in-laws and other members of the family. In such a predicament, the bride often commits suicide. A number of cases of attempted and completed suicides on account of this reason have time and again been highlighted in the press. The horrendous circumstances of torture and pathetic lives of innocent girls all over the country for no fault of their own have attracted the attention of the Government and the public. Although efforts have been made to plug the loopholes in the existing Dowry Prohibition Act, 1961, the evil persists.

In accordance with the statistics available from the 'Accidental Deaths and Suicides in India' published by The National Crime Records Bureau, Ministry of Home Affairs, Government of India, 1992, 80 thousand suicides were reported in the country during 1992. What is still worse, in the decade 1982–92, suicides increased with a high compound growth rate of 6.4 per cent per annum against the population growth 2.1 per cent, thereby resulting in 4.3 per cent growth in the rate of suicides. It further reveals that among the states, West Bengal reported the highest number of suicides, i.e., 16% of the total suicides reported in the country. This was followed by the States of Maharashtra (11.3%), Karnataka (10.2%), Kerala (10.1%) and Tamil Nadu (10.0%).

Next in order were Madhya Pradesh (9.0%) and Andhra Pradesh (8.1%) each contributing more than 5 per cent of the total cases. Among the Union Territories, Delhi and Pondicherry reported sizeable number of cases i.e., 787 and 585 respectively while there was not a single case of suicidal death in Lakshadweep during the year 1992. Similarly, two metropolitan cities, viz., Bangalore and Bombay reported 1.6 per cent and 1.5 per cent of the total suicidal deaths. In other cities the incidence of suicides was, however, less than 1.0 per cent.

There are some important physical and psychological causes which are responsible for suicides. Impotence either physical or psychological is one of the causes of suicide. Likewise, sterility is often the motive of suicide among women. Religious fanaticism also leads to suicide. There are numerous examples of throwing oneself under the wheels of the car of Lord Jagannatha, drowning in the river Ganga, burning one self in the name of religion, fasting till death, etc. In India, poverty and unemployment are important causes for suicides and suicidal attempts. A hungry soul has no charm for life and often resorts to the extreme step of destroying his own self to get rid of his worries and deplorable plight. Of late, the problem of unemployment has assumed an alarming proportion in the country. The present scientific and technological developments have, of course, ushered in new vistas of life, but at the same time these developments have generated an unprecedented tension pervading all spheres of life. As a result people with mental derangements are on the increase. Such mentally deranged persons are generally prone to suicide. A feeling of rejection, a loss of a sense of one's worth, and a sense of total failure in life are common to all potential suicide victims. In some cases of suicides, victims seek to take revenge on parents, friends or other persons who are found to have rejected them. An extreme emotional feeling overtakes them and they feel emotionally isolated from the community.

A person with suicidal tendency needs someone in whom he could confide and off-load some of his apprehensions and problems. If he finds someone who listens to him and gives vent to his feelings, his suicidal tendency gets subsided at least for the time being. It is, therefore, necessary to set up counselling centres in different areas with a board of psychologists, psychiatrists and social workers whose services may be available to them. Some voluntary organisations like Association for Social Health in India have set up family life institutes at different places to provide counselling and guidance to persons with matrimonial problems. On the lines of these institutes, counselling centres for the prevention of suicide may also be established under the auspices of voluntary organisations which are interested in this sphere of social welfare. Persons who have attempted suicide, need psychiatric evaluation and treatment, i.e., psychiatric consultation and follow-up. For those who are potential victims of suicide but have not attempted it, it is necessary to timely detect their mental depression. Generally, individuals with psychoneurotic depression are prone to suicidal attempts. In such cases, not only the individuals but the families should also be educated for the continued care of them until they are fully cured. Therefore, the greatest need for the prevention of suicide is public education and awareness. It should be borne in mind that the individuals who attempt or threaten to commit suicide, are emotionally disturbed persons who are in need of sympathetic professional care. Voluntary mental hygiene organisations are in a better position to help in promoting public education about suicide. An organisation of volunteers 'Sanjivini' is highlighted in the press and reported to have been doing laudable work in helping people with mental and emotional problems. In Great Britain, the suicide rate is said to have gone down ever since the Samaritans came into existence and continued their activities in this field.

In the opinion of Durkheim, the prevention of social isolation and the integration of the individual with a group are the most important tasks for suicide prophylaxis. It is, therefore, necessary to establish contact between lonely people in despair and those who want to help them. Suicide prevention centres at vulnerable areas may undertake the task of informing and educating the public about the problem of suicide through various mass-media like television, radio, newspapers, magazines, etc. The aim of such centre should be to eliminate all factors which tend to increase the incidence of suicides and to strengthen resources congenial for its reduction. Improvement of the existing medical and social services may also contribute towards reduction of the incidence of suicides. There are some social and emotional factors like preservation of family ties, active membership of a social group, good mental and physical health, full employment, etc., which must be taken into consideration while drawing up any programme of suicide prevention.

It is essential to involve members of the community in the planning, organisation and maintenance of an all-embracing scheme for mitigating the problem of suicide. The scientific and technological developments have, of late, ushered in a new era but this progress should be matched with a revolutionary change in social living. Society should not only progress materially but psychologically as well. A mental health movement may be initiated at the national level and a National Institute of Mental Health set up for training personnel and conducting research in the field of suicide prevention. The same institute may have a network of services in various States and Union Territories. In fact, the programme of suicide prevention should contain a multidisciplinary approach including psychology, psychiatry, social work, theology, sociology, anthropology, philosophy, forensic medicine, etc. Voluntary social workers can do a great deal in motivating the community towards the preventive programme of suicide.

END NOTES

1. Durkheim, Emile: *Suicide*, New York, The Free Press, 1966.
2. Douglass, Jack D: *Social Meaning of Suicide*, Princeton, Princeton University Press, 1967.
3. Giddens, Anthony: *The Sociology of Suicide*, Frank Cars & Co. Ltd., 1971.
4. Henry, Andrew F. and Shot, James F: *Suicide and Homicide: Some Economic, Sociological and Psychological aspects of Aggression*, Glancoe, The Free Press, 1954.
5. Morselli, Enrico: Il *Suicidio*, Milano: Dumolard, 1879.
6. Menninger, Karl: *Man Against Himself*, Harcourt, Brace & Co., New York, 1938.
7. *Shneidman* Edwin S. and Farberow Norman L.: *Clues to Suicide*, New York, McGraw Hill Book Co., Inc., 1957.

8. Stengel, Erwin: *Suicide and Attempted Suicide*, Middlesex, England, Penguin Books, 1969.
9. Thakur Upendra: *The History of Suicide in India*, New Delhi, Munshiram Manoharlal Publishers Pvt. Ltd. 1963.
10. Varma, Paripurnanand: *Suicide in India and Abroad*, Agra, Sahitya Bhavan, 1976.
11. Zilboorg, Gregory: 'Considerations on Suicide with particular refrence to 'that of the young', *American Journal of Orthopsychiatry*, Vol. VIII, 1937.

Chapter 11

SUICIDE AND ABETMENT TO SUICIDE

*K. Kumar**

VIJAYLAKSHMI,[1] THE mother of two sons aged 13 and 6 years and two daughters aged 9 and 4 years allegedly caused the death of her two daughters by throwing them into a well, consequent to which they died of asphyxia, attempted to cause the death of her son aged 6 years by throwing into the well and thereafter herself jumped into the well. She and her son were rescued alive and were saved from meeting the watery grave. She was charged for offences punishable under Section 302 I.P.C., for causing the death of her daughters, under Section 307 for having attempted to kill her son and under Section 309 I.P.C. for attempting to commit suicide. The Trial Court awarded imprisonment for life, three years and one year respectively on these accounts. The incident took place on 6.5.1985, presumably due to dire poverty leading to the starvation of the whole family. The mother exhausted her patience at the sight of the starvation of her young children.

In appeal before the High Court of Madras, the Court rather took a lenient view of the matter and sentenced her under Section 304, Part I and held that the period of sentence of 6 years and 9 months, already undergone by her was sufficient to meet the ends of justice and allowed her be released from the prison to enable her to join her husband and son, straight from the Court room, to lead as much comfortable life as is possible within means, which over the years

* Advocate, Supreme Court of India.

had improved. Justice Arunachalam, speaking for the Bench observed:

> This is an unfortunate case where a crime on account of poverty, has led to two young lives meeting their ends, in an unfortunate manner, having been thrown inside a well by the very mother who brought them into this world. Sometimes poverty and starvation lead to parents, not wanting their children to suffer, attempting to put an end to their lives knowing fully well that it is contrary to law. Rhyme or reason does not enter into their minds and they suffer from a phobia, that by killing them, they would achieve their object of putting an end to the sufferings of the children, little realising that sufferings in its true sense, is to commence only thereafter. These are all ways of the world and, while appreciating evidence, in a case of this nature, the Court is bound to have a broad perspective of the entire circumstances, which has led to the unfortunate event. Merely because death was gruesome, one cannot rush to the conclusion that the offence is murder simpliciter or, at the same time, on unfounded or misplaced sympathy, one should not abruptly conclude, that the offence did not amount to murder. The Court is burdened with an onerous duty, of arriving at a conclusion, on the nature of offence committed, taking in entirety, the total evidence placed before it for consideration by the prosecution and the defence.

Earlier in a case[2] of similar nature Justice David Annoussamy, speaking on behalf of the Bench remarked:

> In fact the circumstances of the case are very peculiar to India. Almost every week one can read in the newspaper, the sad story of a mother committing suicide alongwith her children. It looks as if the mother, as a corollary to her duty to nurse the children considers it as a duty not to abandon her progeny. When she has decided to meet death, she hardly reconciles with the idea of dying leaving the children behind.

The learned Judge further stated:

> Usually the unfortunate mother succeeds fully, in her attempt, and the matter does not reach the Court but in rare cases, where courts are seized with such a problem of decision, it has to be taken as to the true nature of offence committed by the mother, who continues to survive, though against her will.

Suicide Defined

Thus suicide, which has been defined as the intentional taking of one's own life[3] is not a crime in the strict sense of the term. The causes of suicide are many, for instance mental diseases and imbalances, unbearable physical ailments, affliction by socially dreaded diseases, decrepit physical conditions disabling the person from taking normal care of the body and performing the normal chores, the loss of all senses or of desire for the pleasures of any of the senses, extremely cruel or unbearable conditions of life making it painful to live, a sense of shame or disgrace or a need to defend one's honour or a sheer loss of interest in life or disenchantment with it, or a sense of fulfilment of the purpose for which one was born with nothing more left to do or to be achieved and a genuine urge to quit the world at the proper moment.[4]

Suicide was prescribed for heinous sex crimes and several other crimes.[5] For many sins, it was ordained that sinner should commit suicide through intake of hot water hot milk or hot butter.[6]

Modes of Suicides Permitted by Scriptures

The Hindu scriptures have prescribed four ways of self destruction, viz., *Bhrigupattan* (to jump down the hill), *Agnidah* (to jump into fire), *Anshan* (fast unto death) and *Ambubhi* (death through drowning).[7] Suicide then was permitted only for expiation of sins, otherwise it was prohibited and any suicide outside these, attracts impurity to the family. It also deprived the person committing suicide to any of the rites meant for the happiness of the soul. *Sati* was one form of suicide by widows by voluntarily burning on the funeral pyre of the husband. This practice was banned by William Bentick.

During Muslim periods the system of *Johar* (mass suicide or self immolation) of ladies from royal families became prevalent in order to avoid being dishonoured by the enemies.

The law does not prescribe any punishment for commission of suicide but an unsuccessful attempt to commit suicide is a punishable offence under Section 309 I.P.C. and punishment for it, may extend to one year simple imprisonment, or with fine, or with both. Section 309 I.P.C. has been struck down as unconstitutional and violative of Articles 14 and 21 of the Constitution of India before the High Courts of A.P.[8], Bombay[9] and Delhi.[10]

Finally, the Supreme Court in *P. Rathinam/Nagahbushan Patnaik* v. *Union of India*[11] has struck it down as violative of Article 21 of the constitution holding that it deserves to be effaced from the statute book.

Abetment of Suicide

However, consequent upon successful commission of suicide, the law-enforcing agencies are not expected to treat the matter as closed because when a valuable life is lost, investigation is required to be done to ascertain the cause of the suicide as well as to find out the person who abetted the suicide. Section 305 provides punishment with death or imprisonment for life, or imprisonment for a term not exceeding ten years for the abetment of suicide by a child or insane person. Section 306 provides punishment with imprisonment of either description for a term which may extend to ten years for a person who abets suicide generally.

Sati is yet a form of suicide which is very much prevalent in the State of Rajasthan and in some cases, the widow is brain-washed, induced and, at times, forced to get burnt on the funeral pyre of the husband and embrace the painful death. The incidence of commission of *Sati* by Roop Kunwar in Deorala village attracted the attention of the press[12] which ultimately resulted in the passing of an Act—The Commission of Sati (Prevention) Act, 1987. Section 4 of the Act says:

4. *Abetment of Sati*—(1) Notwithstanding anything contained in the Indian Penal Code (45 of 1860), if any person commits *sati*, whoever abets the commission of *sati*, either directly or indirectly, shall be punishable with death or imprisonment for life and also be liable to fine.

(2) If any person attempts to commit *sati*, whoever abets such attempt either directly or indirectly, shall be punishable with imprisonment for life and shall also be liable to fine.

Explanation—For the purposes of this Section, any of the following acts or the like shall also be deemed to be an abetment, namely:

(a) any inducement to a widow or women to get her burnt alive alongwith the body of her deceased husband or with any other relative or with any article, object or thing associated with the husband or such relative irrespective of whether she is in a fit state of mind or is labouring under a state of intoxication or stupefaction or other cause impeding the exercise of her free will;

(b) making a widow believe that the commission of *sati* would result in some spiritual benefit to her or her deceased husband or with any other relative or the general well-being of the family;

(c) encouraging a widow or woman to remain fixed in her resolve to commit *sati* and thus instigate her to commit *sati*;

(d) participating in any procession in connection with the commission of *sati* or aiding the widow or woman in her decision to commit *sati* by taking her along with the body of her husband or relation to the cremation or burial ground;

(e) being present at the place where *sati* is committed as an active participant to such commission or to any ceremony concerned with it;

(f) preventing or obstructing the widow or woman from saving herself from being burnt or buried alive;

(g) obstructing or interfering with the police in the discharge of its duties of taking any step to prevent the commission of *sati*.

The expression "abetment" as defined in Section 107 I.P.C. states that a person abets the doing of a thing, who:

(1) instigates any person to do that thing, or (2) engages with one or more other person or persons in conspiracy for the doing of that thing, if an act or illegal omission takes place in persuance of that conspiracy, and in order to the doing of that thing; or (3) intentionally aids by the act or illegal omission, the doing of that thing.

Explanation 1 to the Section, states that a person who, by wilful concealment of material fact which he is bound to disclose, voluntarily causes or procures, or attempts to cause or procure, a thing to be done, is said *to instigate the doing of that thing*.

Explanation 2 to the same Section, states that whoever, either prior to or at the time of the commission of that act, does anything in order to facilitate the commission of that act, and thereby facilitates the commission thereof, *is said to aid the doing of that act*.

A combined reading of Sections 306 and 107 makes it clear that if any person instigates any other person to commit suicide and as a result of such instigation, the other person commits suicide, the person causing the instigation is liable to be punished under Section 306 of the Indian Penal Code for abetting the commission of suicide. A plain reading of this provision shows that before a person can be convicted of abetting the suicide of any other person, it must be established that such other person committed suicide.[13]

Implications of Section 306 read with Section 498A/304B/107 I.P.C. and 113B Evidence Act

Under Section 306 I.P.C., whoever abets the commission of suicide shall be punished with imprisonment which may extend to ten years, if suicide has been committed. Section 498A was inserted in the I.P.C. through Act 46 of 1983. It provides punishment to the husband and/or relatives of the husband of a woman who was subjected to cruelty by them. What is meant by "cruelty" as per the Section has been explained in the Explanation to the Section which reads thus:

"Explanation—For the purposes of this Section, "Cruelty" means:

> (a) any wilful conduct which is of such a nature as is likely to drive the woman to commit suicide or to cause grave injury or danger to life, limb or health (whether mental or physical) of the woman; or
>
> (b) harassment of the woman where such harassment is with a view to coercing her or any person related to her to meet any unlawful demand for any property or valuable security or is on account of failure by her or any person related to her to meet such demand.

The above Explanation consists of two alternative postulates and either of the alternatives would amount to "cruelty". In this context, it is necessary to mention two other provisions incorporated through the same Amendment Act 46 of 1983. One of them is Section 304B of the Penal Code and the other is Section 113B of the Indian Evidence Act Section 304B provides that when death of a woman is caused by any burns or bodily injury or occurs otherwise than under normal circumstances within seven years of marriage such death shall be called "dowry death", if it is shown that soon before her death, she was subjected to cruelty or harassment by her husband or any relative of the husband for or in connection with any demand for dowry. Section 113B of the Evidence Act provides that the Court shall presume that such person has caused the dowry death.

A reading of the aforesaid would indicate that explanation (b) to Section 498A of the Penal Code is the associate of Section 304B of the Penal Code and in such a case Section 113B of the Indian Evidence Act would apply. But Explanation (a) to Section 498A of the Penal code has no such association with any other provision. It stands by itself. In other words, in the case to which Section 498A read with Explanation (b) applies, it would automatically escalate to Section 304B, if death of the woman has occurred within seven years of her marriage otherwise than under normal circumstances. Hence a Magistrate would be justified in converting the case in such a situation into committal proceedings.

But such automatic escalation does not happen in a case to which Explanation (a) to Section 498A applies. In order to constitute the offence under Section 306 of the Penal Code, there should have been abetment of commission of suicide. Section 107 of the Penal code says that a person abets the doing of a thing who either instigates any person to do that thing or engages in a conspiracy for the doing of that thing or intentionally aids the doing of that thing. What is meant by aiding has been clarified vide Explanation 2 to Section 107 I.P.C. (see above).

It is, therefore, clear that an accused against whom the offence under Section 498A I.P.C. is alleged with reference to clause (a) of the Explanation would not automatically become guilty under Section 306 I.P.C. merely because the victim committed suicide even assuming that she did so under the stress of such cruelty. The person, who subjected her to cruelty cannot be deemed to have intentionally aided her to commit suicide. The most which could be found, perhaps, is that she decided to end her life on account of the unbearable cruel treatment meted out to her by such persons. Even then Section 306 I.P.C. cannot be rolled over them.[14]

A reference may be made of some cases in this context. In *Rajan* v. *State of Kerala* the deceased Mohan, was got employed through the efforts of his maternal brother, Ram Babu. Mohan committed theft of some valuables belonging to one Shri Bhagwan Singh Nathwat. The conduct of Mohan shocked Ram Babu. He and Gautam Raj took Mohan to his father in the village and narrated the entire story to him and while doing so he told Mohan:

"You are related to me. You have disgraced me. Your death would have been better than this."

Mohan jumped into the well and died. The appellants were charged for having committed abetment to suicide. The High Court, in revision petition by the appellants, held that the act of committing suicide by Mohan could not be considered as having any proximity or as a consequence or result of uttering any words by the accused persons.[15]

On the other hand, in Romesh Rana Ubale the appellants were convicted by the Additional Sessions Judge, Nasik for commission of offences punishable under Section 396/498A I.P.C. for having abetted the commission of suicide by Ranjana through perpetration of cruelty. The appellants went before the High court in appeal. Upholding the conviction, the High Court observed:[16]

> The fact remains that Ranjana died as a result of having committed suicide after having consumed poison. The question that arises for determination is whether it was the wilful conduct on the part of the accused which prompted Ranjana to commit suicide. The question is not difficult to answer having discussed the evidence in detail. The conduct of the accused Ramesh was of such a nature which drove Ranjana to commit suicide. He subjected his wife to cruelty by beating her under the influence of liquor. The accused went further to humiliate his wife by untying her sari or pressing her neck. In such a condition the cruelty inflicted by accused Ramesh on Ranjana had reached to such a stage that she ultimately committed suicide.

END NOTES

1. *Vijaylakshmi* v. *State of Tamilnadu*, I(1993), CCR 451(DB).
2. *Suyambukkani* v. *State of Tamilnadu*, 1984 L.W. (Ori) 86.
3. *Encyclopedia of Crime and Justice*, Vol. IV, p 1521 (1983 ed).

4. *Maruti Shripati Dubal* v. *State of Maharashtra*, 1987, Cr. L.J. 743.
5. *Dashkumar Charitam*—cited in *Social Problems and Social Disorganisation in India*, C.B. Mamoria, p. 948: *Shabd Kalpdrum Series, Benares*, 1961, p. 321, cited in *Ibid*, p. 949.
6. *Hemadri Prayaschit Khand*, 920, cited in *Ibid*, p. 949.
7. *Amarkosh, Bombay Sanskrit Series*, 1918—cited in *Ibid*, p. 949.
8. *C. Jagadeeswar* v. *State of A.P.*, 1988 Cr. L.J. 549.
9. *Supra* note 4.
10. *State* v. *Sanjay Kumar*, 1985 Cr. L.J. 931 (Delhi).
11. *II(1994) CCR* 351(SC): 1994 Cr. L.J. 1605.
12. Indrajit Badhwar, "Sati—a Pagan Sacrifice, *India Today*, Oct. 15, 1987, pp. 98–105.
13. *Wazir Chand & Another* v. *State of Haryana*, AIR 1989 SC 378.
14. *Rajan* v. *State of Kerala*, II(1994) CCR 1265.
15. *Gautam Raj Mehta* v. *State of Rajasthan* with *Ram Babu Sharma* v. *State of Rajasthan*, 1984 Cr. L.J. 646 (Raj).
16. *Ramesh Rana Ubale* v. *The State of Maharashtra*, II(1995) CCR 1440.

Chapter 12

TECHNOLOGY ADVANCEMENT AS CAUSAL FACTOR OF SUICIDE—A CASE FOR SEEKING PREVENTIVE MEASURES

*Bharat Bhushan Parsoon**

IN THE later half of 20th century science and technology has developed at a faster rate. The techniques being applied for production in the industrial sector have made the man nothing less than a machine. A sort of modernity has operculated in man's functioning where everything has become 'material'. The computers have made the process still more complicated. Bacon, the harbinger of the new age, said that it is the moderns who have achieved a greater knowledge than the relatively young 'ancient world' could have at its disposal. Such comment have made the human being more conscious of achieving rather than contentment. The rat race to outsmart one another and extract maximum out of the existing facilities have increased the ambitiousness of man to become the super-man; thus implying the spirit of self-distruction if the ambitions are not achieved.

The self-destruction or killing one's own self is termed as suicide. The tendencies of committing suicide are indicators of one's alienation, tension and other psychic disorders. A few characteristics of people who commit suicide are

— People of all socio-economic classes commit suicide.

* Additional District and Session Judge, Kurukshetra.

— Loss of money, financial reverses, ill health, unrequitted love, non-achievement of the set goals are frequently given as the cause.
— Women make more suicide attempts, but men commit more suicides. These differences may relate to choices of instruments for suicide - women by an overdose of drugs, men by shooting themselves.
— The rate of suicide is highest among divorced people and next highest among those who are widowed or single.
— The tendency to attempt suicide generally increases with age, but children, adolescents and young adults present an increasing problem.
— The rate of suicide is twice as high among college students as among young people of the same age not in colleges.
— Suicide rate is relatively high among doctors, dentists, lawyers and members of armed forces.
— Suicide increases during economic depressions in the country.

Escapism and suicide

The suicide provides an escape from intolerable external or internal stress; that is suffering from a lingering, painful illness, extreme unhappiness, or irreducible guilt over perceived wrongs committed in the past. Unable to visualise any way that they or anyone else can improve the situation, they resort to suicide as a means of escaping the intolerable stress.

The degree to which the suicidal person sees his situation as hopeless is an important variable in the proclivity towards suicide. Minkoff (1973) found in his study that the people who had attempted suicide had a significant relation between the seriousness of suicide attempt and the level of hopelessness.

Some suicides are motivated by the thought of the effect their death will have on other people. Sometime the desired effect involves retaliation through induction of guilt. "They will be sorry for how they treated me after I am dead". At other times love or attention are the effects wanted.

Stengel (1968) indicates that suicidal motivation is always ambivalent, engaging both the wishes to love and wishes to die. If there is a wish to live, why try to commit suicide? The answer to this question may be that suicidal individuals lack the resources to cope in any other way with the stress or are unaware of external resources that might prove helpful. Some individuals may have the internal resources or knowledge about outside resources but may be too depressed to utilise these resources.

Depression frequently accompanies suicide. The dynamics of suicide and depression are often similar, that is, hopelessness about changing one's life, hostility directed inward, despair etc.

Depression can vary from feeling 'blue' to feeling utterly hopeless and in the grips of despair. The more seriously depressed individuals typically appear sad, discouraged and helpless, have low self esteem, tend to be self critical, have limited interest and show little intiative.

Another characteristic of depressed individual is feeling of anxiety. The way one feels that things should have happened. These persons feel that they deserved better than the treatment being meted out to them. That is how such persons show overt behavior in speech, thought and movement and often gross misappropriation of reality.

What causes depression and anxiety

Depression seems to have a precipitating effect involving loss, separation or new responsibility. However, depression may arise without any apparent triggering external event.

— Technology has led to overproduction and that also at a faster rate. People who are desirous of achievement at a faster rate develop a feeling of accomplishing the goals with the lesser inputs. Sometimes these objectives are not achieved easily. This raises the feeling of loss, that is heightened arousal, greater attachment to the yearned for goals and a diminished ability to relate to available objects or acquire new skills.

— A feeling of attaining money or other aristocracies get in to the individual. He develops a desire to become rich overnight and likes to get the respect being accorded to rich persons.

The modernisation phenomenon has made the woman as equal partner of man with respect to economic set up. Both husband and wife are earning members in a family. This process has made the role of women yearn for career in different professions ultimately taking away the motherly affection from the home. The changes so caused lead to depression. A number of investigators have supported this theses by their studies that depression may result from the physical or emotional separation of an infant from its mother. Spitz (1945) demonstrated that depression was higher in those primates who were separated from their mothers. Harlow (1971) explained this in a statement that once an attachment has been formed, separation results in heightened arousal. Thus bringing the feeling that the world is an empty place but does not affect the individual's self-regard. The depression so caused elicits feelings of self-worthlessness and self-accusation and the depressed person makes little attempt to develop new relationships. According to Freud, the depressed persons not only have ambivalent feeling of love and hate toward the family motherly feeling but also harbour unconscious feeling of rage towards the family members for abandoning them. At the same time such persons develop a feeling of hate against their ownself ultimately leading to murderous feeling of suicide.

Depression is also caused by viewing the others in such conditions that create a pathetic environment. The mass media is often a triggering functionaries in this direction. They enact such social dramas which give the viewers a feeling of poor social response to man's innate feeling of social security. The viewer identifies himself with the character being punished in the social drama. Moss and Boren (1972) will put this situation in a state where manifest depressive behavior is maintained. The depressed individual expresses unhappiness and complaints about the environment causing similar problems to his/her own self. A fear develops in the person and imaginative problems are perceived by him as a part of his life. The common problems of his/her routine life are taken as high potency loss in social system and routine situations are perceived as traumatic events.

The helplessness theory developed by Seligman (1975) postulates that all components of depression—cognitive affective and behavioral, are a result of learning that outcomes (rewards and punishments) are uncontrollable. When people learn that no matter what they do the outcome will be same, they no longer make any adaptive efforts and show the typical symptoms of depression: helplessness and hopelessness. The theory of Seligman holds true in the present day transitional phase of modernity and conventionality. The scientific advancements push the person to think that by his efforts he can achieve the desired goals. But due to conventionality existing in him/her and the environment around him, be is unable to achieve his target, so he develops a feeling of helplessness. He develops a feeling that he is unable to control the environment, unable to achieve the goals, thus a feeling of utter hopelessness.

Most of the abnormal behaviors occur as a consequence of emotional change. Beck (1974) believes that pattern of thinking is the primary symptom in depression. According to him depression is characterised by a negative cognitive set expressed in a negative view of the world and negative expectation of the future. Technological changes, automation and scientific rationalism makes the critical deficiencies. Their environment seems harsh, demanding and depriving. The future also promises more of the same. The depressed person thus assumes personal responsibility for failures and negative outcomes. Also, as depressed individuals become aware of their unhappiness, slowdown in behavior and increased dependency on others, this awareness reinforces their negative expectations of themselves and worsens the depression. In this process, once a negative cognitive set takes effect the depressed person processes information from the outside world in accord with the negative self. In order to accomplish this, he or she distorts reality.

All these factors of depression and anxiety show that learned helplessness and negative thinking as modes of behavior develop because of technological advancement, communication modes, change in social relations, and above all ambitiousness of man. The process of anxiety make the individual rigid, persistent and non-changeable. Some clinical studies of Neuringer (1967) and Salzman and colleagues (1966) help in explaining this process. Laxner (1964) when examined the self-esteem among different groups of psychiatric patients found that depressives had the lowest self-esteem. In other words depressives learn to believe in the uncontrollablility of outcomes. It can also be said in the words of Beck that depressives hold themselves responsible for negative outcomes in order to engage in self-blame. In short it can be said that depression results in the paradoxical situation of individuals blaming themselves for outcomes that they believe they neither caused nor controlled.

Preventive measures

Suicide is a slur on society. It is the responsibility of social system to prevent this menace by helping the individuals to cope-up with the changes of modernity and scientific culture. It can be done in various ways by educating the individuals, making legal provisions and social guidance bureaus.

(a) *Education of Individuals*

Education seeks to decrease the incidence of suicidal behaviours and depression. Publicising the nature of suicide and depression provides the emotional support with practical and social problems.

Educational programmes for physicians, police, welfare workers and others who are likely to come in contact with potential suicides are important. Such groups can be trained to ask questions about possible suicide intent and make referrals to social centres or individuals trained to deal with such problems.

Some special programmes of prevention can be organised for high risk population especially the middle class families who succumb to depression and suicide. Persons from such families are generally more ambitious. Efforts to contact these groups and institute counselling, socialisation, vocational and recreational programmes may reduce the number of depressions and suicides.

Institutional conditions can also contribute to depression and suicide. If the staff of counselling or psychiatric institution are hostile or indifferent, life seems much harsher to visitors and depression increases. Reynolds and Farberow (1976) suggest that when facilities become more humane and more supportive, the quality of life in the institutions improve and suicide is less likely. A humanised setting builds self-esteem and tends to deter suicide. Reynolds and Farberow indicate that such simple staff priorities as talking to patients over a cup of tea, thanking patients for voluntary work and taking the complaints of patients seriously go a long way toward humanising institutional conditions. Sainsbury (1975) studied the suicide rate in England and Wales and found that when hospitals adopted more liberal, open policies in the 1950s suicide among patients declined. On the basis of these findings it can be concluded that championing legislation for more humanitarian institutional care and the institutions of community care should be a step toward lowering the incidence of suicide among mental patients. Sainsbury stresses that institutional change is an important means of prevention.

Another essentiial concomitant of suicide and depression is a sense of powerlessness. No one can control the loss of love in the family or friends circle or some aspect of occupational failure. While everyone has such experiences and becomes atleast mildly and temporarily depressed, some people seem less resilient and become more seriously depressed for a longer period of time. What fosters resilience of such events, that is, the ability to take them in stride? Probably a person's sense of mastery over external and internal events is an important factor. Personal control over one's existence is a significant element in the development of positive self-concept.

Any programme that develops self-reliance and consequently decreases feelings of powerlessness constitutes an educational programme for preventing depression and suicide. Educational programmes that increase vocational skills also help the individual gain a better mastery of environment and can be considered preventive programmes. Another form of prevention is child rearing that encourages children to intiate their own action to bring gratifications and remove annoyances; such an approach may give children a kind of psychological inoculation against a future sense of powerlessness and depression.

In the schools or colleges, the staff of health clinics and student advisement sections should be trained to recognise early symptoms of depression. The staff may then refer students showing such signs to mental health professionals employed by the college or school, or to mental health agencies.

Another potent way out for suicides is education about religion and culture. Faith in God and one's own culture helps in providing strength to the individual. It takes away the feeling of helplessness and hopelessness. The courage picked up after listening to the religious core and sense of calmness can be of great help to suicides.

Most suicides give warning signs that they are going to commit suicide. Many would-be-suicides are willing to talk about their problems. There is need for somebody to listen. Some guidance centres need to be established atleast in educational institutions. The students, no doubt, should be made to understand about how to utilise consultation.

(b) *Social Guidance Bureaus*

In the social system there is need to have suicide prevention centres. These centres should have personnel from various professions. Old persons both males and females can be most helpful. The suicide prevention workers should develop a data base about suicide of particular region. After doing some research and probing realities of causal factors, they should share their feelings and perceptions with others.

Religious centres in the cities and especially the industrial towns should be strengthened. These centres should have some trained religious personnel with whom the people can confer about their problems. Easy access to these centres should be assured on humanitarian grounds. The humane touch and elderly advice of the personnel of these centres can help a lot in providing solace to the individuals.

Legal Provisions

Suicide is a health hazard and speaks about the social health of any society. In the present age of Euthanasia the suicide needs to be looked into from different angle. The individual who commits suicide tries to highlight some of the problems of the society where justice is needed. The legal section of the society should look into the problem which is highlighted rather than thinking of punishing the person who fails to commit suicide. Gandhiji once observed, 'Death is our friend, the truest of friends. He delivers us from agony. I do not want to die of a creeping paralysis of my faculties—a defeated man'. The society should look into the problems of its members and the legal section of the society should investigate the problem highlighted by the act of suicide.

The constitutional provision under Article 21 that word 'life' means right to live with human dignity and does not merely connote continued drudgery has to be taken with its instituted means. That is how the Supreme Court of India in its judgement (1994) has provided that suicide is no more an immoral act. But the question of living in an inhumane style has not been solved by this act. There is need to restructure the judiciary to prevent suicide. A guidance cell on the lines of grievances cell needs to be created in the courts at district level. Every individual should have right to amicable approach these cells and reposite his/her grievances against the society. The elderly persons in the capacity of judges should listen to the problems and then venture to help such individuals.

In short it can be said that depression is a precondition to suicide although most people who are depressed do not take their lives. The major cause of this depression or suicide is the technological advancements. The change in life-style, social relations, environment has made the people sensitive and emotional. Ultimately anxiety and ambitiousness has gripped every individual. Over production and hurry to reach the goal at the earliest have made the individuals impatient. This ultimately gives rise to change in attitude and feeling of helplessness. The only way to avoid these ailments lies in educating the public, training key persons in the community, establishing suicide prevention centres, making legal provisions about dealing with suicides, creating grievances redressal cells in the judiciary etc. A good educationist, humane judge and accomodating society can help a lot in getting over the problem of suicide.

END NOTES

1. Minkoff, K., Bergman.E. and Beck. A.T., "Hopelessness, Depression and Attempted Suicide", *American Journal of Psychology*, 30:455–459, 1973.
2. Stengel, E., 'Attempted Suicide' in H.L. Resnik (ed.) *Suicidal Behaviour.* Boston, Little Brown, 1968.
3. Spitz, R.A., 'Hospitalism: An Inquiry into the Genesis of Psychiatric Conditions in Early Childhood': *Psychoanalytic study of the child*, 1:53–74, 1945.
4. Harlow, H.F., Harlow, M.K. and Suomi, S.J., 'From Thought to Therapy: Lessons from Primate Laboratory'. *American Scientist* 59:538–549, 1971.
5. Moss, G.R. and Boren, J.H., 'Depression as a Model for Behaviour Analysis,' *Comprehensive Psychiatry*, 13: 581–590, 1972.
6. Saligman, M.E.P. "*Hopelessness: On Depression, Development and Death*," San Francisco, W.H. Freeman, 1975.
7. Beck, A.T., "Affective Disorders" in S. Arienti (ed.). *American Handbook of Psychiatry* (2nd ed.) New York, Basic Books, 1974.
8. Neuringer, C. 'The Cognitive Organisation of Meaning in Suicidal Individuals' *Journal of General Psychology*, 26:96–100, 1967
9. Salzman, L. et. al, 'Conceptual thinking in Psychiatric Patients'. *Archives of General Psychiatry*, 14: 55–59, 1966.
10. Laxner, R.M., "Self Concept Changes of Depressive Patients in General Hospital Treatment" *Journal of Consulting Psychology*, 28: 214–219, 1964.
11. Sainsbury, P.,'Community Psychiatry', in S. Perlin (ed.) A Handbook for Study of Suicide, Golan, Oxford University Press, 1975.

Chapter 13

TO BE OR NOT TO BE

*Kanwal Sapra**

Introduction

LIFE IS a divine gift. To preserve it is commendable and to destroy it is condemnable. There is no denying the fact that He who gives life can alone take it—Almighty. Thus, came the Divine command 'Thou shall not kill'; obviously the command is not only not to kill others but also yourself. Therefore, most people cling to life even in adverse circumstances. However, there are individuals who are very emotional, sentimental and are easily overpowered by depression in adverse circumstances. In their moments of depression, they see no charm in life, and seek relief by extinguishing the flame of their life by committing suicide. However, dejection alone is not the ground for suicide. Religious and social grounds are other factors relevant in suicide. In India the history of Vedic age is replete with numerous examples of suicides committed on religious grounds.

The practice of taking samadhi for attaining eternal peace is not unknown to Indian society. Besides religious grounds, social conditions also led to mass suicide such as the practice of committing 'Jauhar' by wives of defeated soldiers and kings to protect their honour from the invaders. The practice of *sati* by women after the death of their husbands is another instance on point.

* Inspector, Delhi Police.

An increasing number of suicides is an alarming situation and a matter of great concern these days. It is a social evil and a threat to mankind and humanity itself as a whole. The human nature differs from person to person. Some of us have strong will power, some have weak and the rest may stand somewhere in between. Accordingly, the degree of strength to sustain the pressures differ from person to person. Certainly, the people with strong or moderate will power, will deprecate or condemn the act of an attempt to commit suicide. They will overcome such a situation while the others may succumb to these pressures.

However, with the technological development, urbanisation of society, degeneration of human values and movement from spiritualism to materialism, peace for men has become uncommon, while stress and strain, depression and dejection has become very common. At least in modern society depression has played a dominant role in the alarming rate of increasing number of suicides. Therefore it is not unusual to see the reports of suicide in daily newspapers.

The malaise of suicide has always been viewed with different angles both religiously and sociologically, some deprecating it and others holding it not blameworthy. Legally it was condemned and with the enactment of Indian Penal Code 1860, attempt to suicide was made punishable. However, inspite of this, like sociological and religious difference that existed, legal difference of opinion as to the validity of law providing punishment for attempt to suicide also emerged and different views were expressed by the High Courts.

However, the matter has now been finally settled by the Supreme Court holding that punishment for attempt to suicide is unconstitutional.

The purpose of this paper is to critically analyse not only the social and religious angulations of suicide but also to critically analyse the judicial view on the point.

Meaning of suicide

Suicide has been defined as an act or instance of taking one's own life voluntarily and intentionally; the deliberate and intentional destruction of one's own life by a person; one that commits or attempts self-murder.[1] It means a person who intentionally kills himself or intentional self-slaughter, or undertaking a mission involving his own death, or action destructive to one's own interests.[2] Durkheim is of the view that the term 'suicide' is applied to any death which is the direct or indirect result of a positive or negative act accomplished by the victim himself.[3]

Reasons for committing/attempting suicide

There are various reasons[4] for committing suicide/attempting suicide—growing population, industrialization and the migration from villages to the urban areas, failure in love affairs or matrimonial life, in business or profession, schizoprenia, poverty, unemployment, sudden change in economic, political, social or religious conditions etc.

Suicide[5] is also committed due to the natural calamities. Official tension has become another cause of committing suicide or attempt to suicide in the present era. It is also committed as an act of revenge against the illtreatment or maltreatment of family members.

Modes of committing suicide

There are numerous methods/modes of committing suicide or attempt to suicide such as, drowning, burning, poisoning, jumping into well, river, sea etc., jumping from high-rise buildings, a cliff or a tree, hanging, fire/self-immolation, electrocution, stabbing, shooting, starvation or fasting[6-7], *Jauhar*,[8] *sati*,[9] overdose of medicines, consuming sleeping pills, pesticides, intoxicating drugs, getting runover by automobiles, trains etc. Consuming potassium cynide generally by the extremists and hardened criminals is increasing day by day which has become an easier and painless mode of committing suicide or attempt to suicide in the modern times. Just as abuse of medication plays a role in suicide, alcohol also frequently plays a role.[10]

Schools of suicide

It is universally known and proved that life is a blend of chemical and biological reactions and has the capacity to bear certain amount of heat, cold, pain, happiness and so on. When any of the factors which is responsible for the sustenance of life is disturbed by way of excessive effect over the body, the system of life is disturbed and life circle is shortened/cut, which is death. Brain is the pivot of life machine and when it starts giving negative signals of maintenance of body, man tends to finish it, due to unbearability of pain, failure of achievement, fear of insults etc. Such type of tolerance is different from man to man. Same type of situation has different effects over the brain. In his 'Paradise Lost', Milton says; "The mind in itself can make a Heaven of Hell, Hell of Heaven."

However, there is no denying the fact that the life of a man is full of sorrows and sufferings these days. Every person lives under strain and stress. It is this and depressed state of mind which incite the man to shorten one's own life to get rid of the numerous problems by committing suicide. However, the problem of suicide raises many questions. Has a person right to die on his own sweet will or otherwise? Do the ethics, traditions, customs, religions permit suicide? Can a relative or friend, or a doctor assist a person, to meet death? Is it a crime? If at all it is a crime then should there be legal punishment for committing suicide?

There are two schools of thought regarding suicide. In Ancient Greek and Roman civilizations, suicide was considered morally blameless and at times desirable and commendable.[11] The Greeks permitted the criminals to put an end to their lives if they were convicted of certain offences. Suicide, like crime is for Durkheim, no indication of immorality per se.[11]

Walter Charleton opined that to vindicate one's self from inevitable calamity by suicide is not a crime.[12] In Japanese culture committing suicide is considered a matter of honour.

Kautilya has condemned those who committed suicide under the infatuation of love, anger, and other sinful passions. The Brahmapurana holds the view that those who commit suicide by poison, fire, hanging, drowning, falling from a cliff or a tree, should be classed with those who commit great sins. The Vishnu Sanhita also condemns such persons. Inspite of condemnations by ancient religious authorities, suicide has continued to be practised since times immemorial.

Society can never expect destruction whether it is of self or other, except by the rule of law as propounded by Dicey, since it would be opposed to the very existence of this society. John Locke was of the same view. Suicide is unnatural,immoral and causes social imbalance of society. Plato and Aristotle condemned it as an act of cowardice. Suicide is a violation of the commandment, opined St. Augustine. St. Thomas Acquinas was of the view that God alone has control over life and death and anyone who decides the moment of his death commits or attempts suicide, usurps God's power.

Christianity has considered suicide as a grave sin and many centuries ago, those who committed suicide were refused a Christian burial unless it could be shown that they were "insane"

Mohamedan societies prohibit suicide with equal vigor. "Man" says Moḥamad, "dies only by the will of God according to the Book which fixes the term of his life.[13]

'Yes' or 'No' of deprival of life—Legal aspects.

Deprival of life can be done by the individual himself and by state also. However, the Constitutional framers were well aware of the important rights of human beings. Accordingly, in one of the precious jewels of our Constitution viz. Article 21, the right to life has been incorporated—a jewel polished and given its due beauty by judicial activism. This article upholds the sanctity of life and enjoins that no one can be deprived of his life except according to procedure established by law. Therefore, the State can deprive its citizen's of its life only by procedure established by law.

But the question is, can an individual deprive himself of his life? In this regard Section 309 of the Indian Penal Code, 1860 makes attempt to suicide punishable with simple imprisonment for a term which may extend to one year or with fine or with both. This provision incorporates one of the state's interest i.e. preventing suicide. The issue whether this provision is constitutional or unconstitutional has attracted the attention of courts.

Judicial attitude

In *Emperor* v. *Musammat Mulia*,[14] a woman, driven almost frantic by pains of prolonged labour attempted to take her own life and in so doing her infant was born dead. She was held guilty of attempting to commit suicide but not of attempting to voluntarily cause miscarriage.

In *Emperor* v. *Dhirajia*,[15] an ill-treated wife, who in endeavouring to escape from her husband jumped into an open well with her baby in her arms was found not guilty for attempted suicide as it was held that the offence was not an attempt to commit suicide in as much as the word 'suicide' in s.309 involves conscious effort.

In *Valentino Esperdio de Souza, Appellant* v. *State, Respondent*,[16] the accused in extreme penury condition jumped into a well together with his 15 months old daughter. The court observed that the accused has to be pitied rather despised as he took the extreme step of attempting to finish his own and his daughter's life as they were dying due to hunger. Accordingly, it was held that the sentence of imprisonment already undergone by him under Section 309 I.P.C. would meet the ends of justice. The court recommended to the Government for remission of sentence.

In *Chenna Jagadeeswar* v. *State of Andhra Pradesh*,[17] it was held that Section 309 I.P.C. is valid and does not offend Articles 19 and 21 of the Constitution of India. The court also observed that it is rather difficult to hold that the right to life impliedly guaranteed by the Constitution of India includes the right to die. Further, if Section 309 I.P.C. is to be held illegal, it is highly doubtful whether Section 306 I.P.C. could survive. Thus, people who actively assist and induce persons to commit suicide may go scot free.

It is important to note that the court observed that it is a paradox that society will neither provide sustenance nor allow the sufferer to die. In this complexity of social maladjustments, the best safeguard is that the Court should exercise and tamper its judgement with humanity and compassion.

In *State, Appellant* v. *Sanjay Kumar Bhatia*,[18] the court deprecated the existence of the provision by observing that it is ironic that Section 309 I.P.C. still continues to be on our Penal Code. It was observed that the continuance of Section 309 I.P.C. is an anachronism unworthy of a human society like ours.

The Delhi High Court in *Court on its own motion* v. *Yogesh Sharma*,[19] displayed yet another form of judicial response which not only deemed all the prosecutions for an offence under Section 309 I.P.C, outright unjust but positively detrimental to the rule of law notion itself.

The court concluded that it is quite clear that there is a total non-application of mind when starting prosecution under Section 309 I.P.C. To allow such prosecution to drag on for years when the victims have had enough of misery and when the accused also belong to the poorer sections of the society is to add further insult to the injury and that too at the hands of of the courts.

On the other hand the Bombay High Court in *Maruti Shripati Dubal* v. *Maharashtra*[20] declared Section 309 to be unconstitutional as being violative of Articles 14 and 21 of Indian Constitution. The High Court declared that right to die was part of the personal liberty guaranteed by Article 21 of the Constitution and the impugned section violated it insofar as it made it an offence. It was held that since the right to life contemplates the negative aspect it, therefore, subsumes an individual's fundamental right of self destruction.

Commenting on the case, Prof. D.C. Pande says that it is true that the theme of attempting to commit suicide as an offence suffers from several infirmities.[21] He further says that this decision is potentially filled with numerous controversies and would require further scrutiny by Parliament, judiciary and the press.[22]

This liberal judgement on suicide raises strange issues. Ironically, this can now be interpreted to justify the negation of female life. In other words, will '*sati*' get a fresh lease of life? Even though this liberal judgement will help many, it will unfortunately expose some women to barbaric and inhuman pressures from traditional societies. This judgement can at best give the woman a negative form of power—the power to destroy herself. Will not this judgement work in favour of those who instigate?[23]

There are cases in which existence is totally purposeless, meaningless and painful. Under such circumstances a patient should have the right to choose death over a miserable existence.[24]

The stretching of Article 21 to include the right to die is not only illogical but also antithetical for a full and meaningful realization of the right to life.[25] The court's observation[26] seems to equate the desire to life with the desire to die and locate the origin of both in the free-will of the individual.

Badar Durrez Ahmad[27] says that he would certainly not go so far as to say that every person has a fundamental right to die...The High Court's decision that there is a fundamental right to die is not correct.[28]

In *P. Rathinam* v. *Union of India and Another*,[29] the Supreme Court has held that Section 309 of the Penal Code deserves to be effaced from the statute book to humanise our penal laws. It is a cruel and irrational provision, and it may result in punishing a person again (doubly) who has suffered agony and would be undergoing ignominy because of his failure to commit suicide. An act of suicide cannot be said to be against religion, morality or public policy, and an act of attempted suicide has no baneful effect on society. It was, therefore, held that Section 309 violates Articles 21. Referring to earlier decisions on Article 21 the court held that right to live of which Article 21 speaks can be said to bring in its trail the right not to live a forced life.

The Court was of the view that it would advance not only the cause of humanisation which is a need of the day, but of globalisation also, as by effacing Section 309, this part of the criminal law would be attuned to the global wavelength. In its view this was also in consonance with the recommendation of the Law Commission of India in the 42nd Report (1971).

It was also held that the view that distinction between 'suicide' and 'euthanasia' is logically inconsistent may not be quite incorrect, because in passive euthanasia, wherever it has been accepted as legally permissible, consent of the patient, if he be in a sound mental condition, has been regarded as one of the prerequisites. So, if one could legally commit suicide he could also give consent for his being allowed to die.

Making a distinction between Section 306 and 309 I.P.C., the court said that it is not possible to accept the view that if Section 309 were to be held bad, it is highly doubtful whether Section 306 could survive, as self-killing is conceptually different from abetting others to kill themselves.

The court observed that the question whether Article 21 has positive content or is merely negative in its reach is no longer Res Integra as this court in *Unnikrishnan* v. *State of Andhra Pradesh*[30] (in which right to receive education upto the primary stage has been held to be a call of Article 21) has virtually answered this question. This would appear from what was stated by Mohan J in para 19 and by Jeevan Reddy in para 170. In Paragraph 30 Mohan J has mentioned about the rights which have been held to be covered under Article 21 and these being: the right to go abroad,[31] right to privacy,[32] right against solitary confinement,[33] right against fetters,[34] right to legal aid,[35] right to speedy trial[36], right against handcuffing[37] right against delayed execution,[38] right against custodial violence[39] etc.

The aforesaid is enough to state that Article 21 has enough of positive content in it. The term life means something more than animal existence. This view was accepted by a Constitution Bench of this Court in *Sunil Batra* v. *Delhi Administration*[40] to which further leaves were added in *Board of Trustees Port of Bombay* v. *Dilip Kumar*,[41] *Ram Saran* v. *Union of India*,[42] *State of Himachal Pradesh* v. *Umed Ram*[43] and *CESC Ltd.* v. *Subhash Chandra*.[44]

In these decisions it was held that the word 'life' in Article 21 means right to live with human dignity and the same does not merely connote continued drudgery. It takes within its fold some of the finer graces of human civilisation which makes life worth living and that the expanded concept of life would mean the 'tradition' culture and heritage of the concerned person.

There has been no unanimity in welcoming the controversial pronouncement of the Supreme Court as different views have been expressed on it: Suicide leaves no crime behind. Punishing such a person is a travesty of justice and jurisprudence, even if sanctioned by law[45]; since there is a separate Central Act on sati, even after the abolition of Section 309 of I.P.C., attempt to commit sati would continue to be a punishable offence.[46] It is a long-awaited verdict for the society's good;[47] but does not necessarily make the task of those trying to help suicidal persons any easier;[48] it indeed is a bold step to humanise the legal system;[49] it is historic judgement seeking to "humanise" the criminal law;[50] it is a long-awaited step towards 'humanising' the law, but concern should have been voiced for a need for greater vigilance lest the 'legal sanction' be misused to cover up dowry deaths and other criminal acts;[51] it certainly embarked on a landmark departure from tradition; entering a new and social dimension for concern for the emotionally burdened individual where penal actions only added insult to injury.[52]

It is "a welcome decision" and a "revolutionary judgement", which comes as a welcome reprieve to the unfortunate ones pushed into trying to end their lives and then suffering the embarrassment and agony of being tried;[53] it endorses the essential liberation position that the right to life includes the right to die at a time of one's own choosing.[54] In the historic judgement, Supreme Court has declared as unconstitutional and hence void Section 309 I.P.C., which makes attempt to suicide a punitive offence.[55] The judgement has at least enabled society to see the truth;[56] it will prove to be a milestone in India's judicial history; the judgement will benefit tens of thousands of misserable souls who are prosecuted for failing to kill themselves;[57] it comes as a hope of liberation to some who are in a very depressed and irreversible state of mind or body, without fear of any punishment should their attempt fail.[58]

Rev. Alan de Lastic,[59] commenting on the judgement said though in legal language it may not be considered a crime, morally it still stands unjustified and unacceptable.[60]

The historic judgement, though it may be welcomed by a wide cross-section of society, seems to have erred in ignoring the well-known and well-laid-down theories of the cause-and-effect relationships-found to be valid both over the laws of the materialistic world or physics as well as of psychology, which describes and monitors the human behaviour.[61]

The views of Supreme Court and the High Courts without touching Section 306 is incomplete. In this regard it should be mentioned that interesting studies with regard to criminal liability for assisting suicide have been made in America.[62]

The judicial response on the question of attempt to suicide has been inconsistent. The state response to the persons making attempt to suicide is also inconsistent. Why is Jaya Prada charged with attempted suicide but not Vinoba Bhave or Jain Monks etc. starving themselves to death? Similarly, why the attempted self-immolation bid by two leaders in Delhi was foiled by Delhi Police, who were protesting against the alleged molestation of women and unwarranted police firing on Uttrakhand supporters in Muzaffarnagar in U.P.[63]

The judgement of the Supreme Court will raise a problem in the area of Insurance Law. If the right to live and the right not to live is guaranteed with absolute freedom under Article 21 of the Indian Constitution then a situation may arise where many daring and emotional/sentimental people may choose the latter in order to provide a prosperous and happy life to their dependents.

In *Beresford* v. *Royal Insurance company Limited*,[64] the personal representative of a person, who, having insured his life, committed suicide while sane, was held not entitled to recover the policy money from the Insurance Company, for it would be contrary to public policy to assist a personal representative to recover the fruits of the crime committed by the assured.

If everything in life is absurd, the act of taking one's life merely compounds the meaninglessness of existence.[65]

The Supreme Court did not explicate the related medico-legal issue of euthanasia or mercy killing. The judgement is, therefore, both unsettling and incomplete. It must be hoped that a larger bench will throw light on this complex and sensitive matter before it is too late.

It is interesting to note that subsequent to the upholding of attempt to suicide as unconstitutional in a recent pronouncement in *Vijay @ Gyanchand Jain* v. *The State of Madhya Pradesh*,[66] wherein the accused was convicted, interalia, under Section 309 I.P.C. and sentenced to one year R.I. by the trial court, the conviction and sentence for attempt to suicide was also upheld by the Supreme Court.

The judgement in this case is per incuriam as it makes no reference to *P. Rathinam's* case. However, it is not clear whether ommission to reject P. Rathinam's judgement[67] is intentional or inadvertent. Consequently, the uncertainty has become a problem for the law enforcement agencies, whether the person who attempts to commit suicide should be prosecuted or not?[67]

In recent times, the Western societies have shown a substantial and remarkable change in their attitude towards the suicidal tendencies of an individual. Such an individual is looked upon as the one requiring help and guidance.[68]

English common law held suicide to be a serious crime. It was viewed as an offence, not only against God and nature, but against the king, who was thereby deprived of his subject. The penalty varied depending on the motive for the suicide. If the suicide was motivated by anger or illwill, land and chattels were forfeited to the king.

In *Kirkham* v. *Chief Constable of the Greater Manchester Police*,[69] the court emphasised the duty of the police to take care of persons in custody with suicidal tendencies.[70] In cases where it is doubtful that the case was of suicide or homicide it has been held that suicide must be proved by evidence, and if it is not proved by evidence, it is the duty of the coroner not to find suicide, but to find an open verdict.[71] It is to be ascertained during investigation of an incident whether the case is of homicide or suicide.

United Kingdom set the pace by enacting the Suicide Act of 1961. Whereas previously suicide was regarded as a serious felony, requiring burial in a public highway, and forfeiture of properties of the deceased, it laid-down that suicide was no longer to be regarded an offence. The Act does more than abolish the crime of suicide. It is symptomatic of a change in the public attitude to suicide generally... The fact that aiding and abetting suicide remains a crime under Section 2 of the said Act does not diminish the force of the argument.

In the United States and USSR attempted suicide is not a crime. There exists no legal right to commit or to assist in committing the act of suicide.[72]

Conclusions and suggestions

To be or not to be is a Hobson's choice! The problem of suicide has attracted the attention of philosophers and religious heads, some holding it against the divine will and the others holding it not morally condemnable. Though attempt to commit suicide was made a punishable offence under Indian Penal Code, 1860, yet this provision was a centre of controversy, a fact which is evident from differing pronouncements of various High courts.

Some High Courts taking the view that right to life under Article 21 of the constitution, includes right to die, while the others holding that it does not include so.

The curtain was dropped finally by the Supreme Court when it, in the name of humanising the law, struck down the provision as unconstitutional. However, this pronouncement has not considered many questions. For example, it will lead to revival of social evils already eradicated such as, *Sati* and *Jauhar*. While the main offence has been declared unconstitutional, abetment and assisting to commit suicide still remains on the statute book. The judgement has not given its nod to another important feature of the problem related to suicide i.e. euthanasia.

It will have also its impact on Insurance law because financially crippled persons will commit suicide in order to benefit their survivors.

The effect or impact of judgement on the society has not been taken into account by the court because it would be a controversial question as to whether a man has a duty to prevent a person from committing suicide. Should a police officer, who is equally a part of the modern welfare State, be a mere spectator to an incident of suicide which is being committed just in front of him? Whosoever commits suicide by leaving a note or otherwise, causes lot of problems to his survivors i.e. dependents, relatives, family members, friends, etc. It clearly shows that when a person commits suicide, it affects others. The question of live or not to live might be personal matter but it does affect the society at large.

The irresistible consequence of the judgement is, "give me what I want—no matter right or wrong or else I commit suicide."

The provision has been held unconstitutional in the name of humanising the law. However, the better option would have been to humanise the sentence i.e. the conviction should have been upheld but a humane view should have been taken while imposing the sentence.

In an era, when a view is gaining ground that the State should not extinguish the flame of an individual's life by imposing death penalty, is it not unfortunate for the judiciary to give a licence to individuals themselves to commit suicide?

Suicide can not be taken up as the method of controlling the population. Even efforts made by the State to prevent attempts to suicide reveal inconsistent views. Double standard by State is deprecative in this regard.

The effacing of the provisions of Section 309 I.P.C. from the statute book will pave the way for dowry seekers in easily creating circumstances for the brides to commit suicide.

Can we ultimately attain the object of establishing Human Rights Commission by holding right to die rather than compelling the State to preserve human life with its due dignity?

Keeping in view the Supreme Court judgement, the question arises: is it right for the State to hold the view that those who are unable to live a dignified life are welcome to depart?

In modern democratic states, the welfare of the general public should be given importance. It is therefore the duty of the State to make every endeavour to preserve human life.

It is also suggested to provide all help—economic, moral, social, etc.—to such a person by the family members, friends etc. There should be advisory and legal councils of independent private organizations. The government should also extend all possible help and moral courage. A person accused of attempting to commit suicide should be sent to some welfare homes and not be discarded. Such persons require the help of a psychiatrist instead of prison sentence.

Assuming that a man who attempts suicide does so by reason of the fact that he is a victim of the society, the correct course is to rehabilitate him back in the society by counselling, giving him necessary assistance, psychiatric treatment instead of giving him a carte blanche to end his life.

For having a better view of the problems of suicide scientific research should also be conducted so that the reasons for committing suicides could be ascertained and preventive action taken accordingly by the authorities. State takes care of the juvenile delinquents, exploited women, and its aged and neglected citizens, by opening juvenile homes, Nari Niketan etc. Similar efforts should also be made for persons with suicidal tendencies. By judicial activism the right to life has been made really meaningful. However, it is unfortunate that a right to die has also been read into Article 21.

END NOTES

1. *McKay v. Bergstedt*, 106 Nev. 820, 801, at 625 (1990), cited in '*Suffolk University Law Review*', Vol. XXV, No. 3, Fall, 1991, p. 83.
2. See, The concise Oxford Dictionary, Sixth Edition, Edited by J.B. Sykes, Delhi, Oxford University Press, Bombay; Calcutta, Madras, 1976, (1977–1980); see generally; Warton's Law Lexicon, Fourteenth Edition, Sweet & Maxwell, Universal Book Traders, Second Indian Reprint, 1994, (Stating that suicide means self slaughter); The concise Oxford Dictionary–The New Edition–1990s, Eighth Edition, Edited by R.E. Allen, Delhi, Oxford University Press (Stating that suicide means the intentional killing of oneself or self destructive action); The Advance Learner's Dictionary of current English, Second Edition, The English Language Book Society And Oxford University Press, 1963, Printed in Great Britain (Stating that suicide means crime of self murder); Legal Glossary 1988, Law & Justice Ministry, Govt. of India (Stating that suicide means self-slaughter or self-destruction); and L.B. Curzon—A Dictionary of Law, Macdonald & Evans, Reprinted, 1982 (Stating that suicide means the taking of one's own life intentionally and voluntarily).
3. Emile Durkheim, "*Suicide—A Study in Sociology*", translated by John A. Spaulding and George Simpson, Edited with an Introduction by George Simpson, The Free Press, New York, Collier-Macmillan Limited, London.
4. For an interesting study on the causes of committing/attempting suicide, see, *The Times of India*, 7.5.94, under the caption, "Tomorrow's Zero-Suicide, Society And The Individual", by Jug Suraiya; see also, Accidental Deaths and Suicides in India, 1987, National Crime Records Bureau, Ministry of Home Affairs, Government of India.
5. For an interesting study on 'suicide' with reference to sex, age, region, economic condition, education etc., see, Rajendra Pandey, "Suicide and Social Structure in India", pp. 5–29, *Social Defence*, Vol. XXI, No. 83, January 1986.

6–7. Vinoba Bhave, the great disciple of Mahatma Gandhi adopted the method of starving/fasting and left the world. The then prime Minister Mrs. Indira Gandhi even could not prevent him from doing so. Many saints/Rishis who were Hindus and Jains adopted the same method of leaving the world and the society didn't consider the same as suicide. For an interesting study on starving or fasting to death, see, *The Hindustan Times*, 19.5.94 under the caption, "Attempted suicide not punishable", by Arvind Kala.

8. Generally, Rajput women used to immolate themselves after the defeat of the King in a war, in order not to fall in the clutches of foreign invaders. Rani Padmini set an example of such a heroic self-sacrifice when she alongwith hundreds of other Rajput women voluntarily immolated herself, rather than be touched by the foreign invaders who had won the Chittaur. For an excellent and interesting study on the topic, see, *The Hindu*, Madras, 14.6.94, under the caption, "A real blot on penal law removed" by C. Achutha Menon; For religious mass suicide in Switzerland see generally, *The Times of India*, New Delhi, 6.10.94, under the caption, "Mass suicide by religious Sect"; see also, *Indian Express*, 7.10.94, under the caption, "Cult suicide leaves Swiss shell-shocked", by Chitra Subramaniam; *Time-International*, No. 42, October 17, 1994, p. 30, under the caption, "Despite the signs of murder, at least some of the deaths may be suicides, an episode in cult pathology to put beside Jonestown and Waco"; and *Newsweek, The International News Magazine*, pp. 38–43, October 17, 1994, "Suicide Cult".

9. For an interesting study on the issue of '*Sati*' see, S.K. Bhattacharya "Suicide", p. 21, *Social Defence*, Vol. XIX, No. 76, April 1984. *The Times of India*, May 27, 1994, under the caption, "*Sati attempt still punishable.*"

10. See e.g. *Mallet* v. *Louisiana Nursing Homes*, Inc; 459 So. 2d 178 (La. Ct. App. 1984), cited in *Drake Law Review*, Vol. 39, No. 1, 1989–1990, p. 136.

11. *Supra. note 3 at 16.*

12. S.K. Bhattacharya, "Suicide", p. 21, *Social Defence*, Vol. XIX, No. 76, April 1984.

13. *Korán*, III, v. 139, cited in emile Durkheim, "*Suicide—A study in sociology*" p. 329, translated by John. A. spaulding and George simpson edited with an introduction by george Simpson, The Free Press, New York, Collier-Macmillan Limited London.

14. (1919) 20 Cri. L.J. 395 (all).

15. AIR 1940 All 386.

16. AIR 1967 Goa, Daman and Diu 138.

17. 1987(2) A.L.T. 263; 1988 Cri. L.J. 549 (AP).

18. (1985) Cri. L.J. 931 (Delhi).

19. Cri. Review No. 230 of 1985 (Del.) and unreported High Court Decision delivered by Chief Justice Rajindar Sachar on 13.12.1985.

20. (1986) Mah. L.J. 913 (Bom.); 1987 Cri. L.J. 713 (Bom.).: (1986) 88 Bom. L.R. 589.

21. D.C. Pandey, Research Professor, OLI, p. 266, *Annual Survey of Indian Law*, Vol. XXIII, 1987.
22. *Id.* at p. 265.
23. Editorial Notes, "Taking one's life", p. XXXVIII, *Calcutta Weekly Notes*, Vol. XCI, November 1986 to 1987, Part 13, Monday, February 16, 1987. p. XXXVIII.
24. *Ibid.*
25. B.B. Pande, Reader in Law, University of Delhi, "Creating A Right to Die-an Exercise in futility", p. 117, *Islamic and Comparative law Quarterly*, Vol. VII, No. I, March 1987.
26. *Id.* at p. 118; the court's observation is, "there is nothing unnatural about the desire to die and hence with the right to die. Whatever the circumstances which induce a person to end or terminate his or her life the act of termination of life is the act of that individual. It is no less his than his act of living".
27. Advocate, Supreme Court of India.
28. "Organ Transplant And The Right To Die", p. 126. *Islamic And comparative Law Quarterly, Vol. VII*, No. 1, March, 1987.
29. 1994(3) SCC 394.
30. 1993(1) SCC 645.
31. *Satwant Singh Sawhney* v. *D. Ramanathnan, APO, New Delhi*. AIR 1967 SC 1836.
32. *Govind* v. *State of MP*, (1975) 2 SCC 148.
33. *Sunil Batra* v. *Delhi Admn.*, (1978) 4 SCC 494.
34. *Charles Shobraj* v. *Supdt. Central Jail*, (1978) 4 SCC 104.
35. *M.H. Hoskot* v. *State of Maharashtra*, (1978) 3 SCC 544.
36. *Hussainara Khatoon* v. *Home Secy. State of Bihar*, (1980) 1 SCC 81.
37. *Prem Shankar Shukla* v. *Delhi Admn.*, (1980) 3 SCC 526.
38. *T.V. Vatheeswaran* v. *State of TN*, AIR 1983 SC 361.
39. *Sheela Barse* v. *State of Maharashtra*, (1983) 2 SCC 96.
40. AIR 1978 SC 1675.
41. AIR 1983 SC 109.
42. AIR 1989 SC 549.
43. AIR 1986 SC 847.
44. 1992(1) SCC 441.
45. 14.6.94, "A real blot on penal law removed," by C. Achuta Menon.
46. *The Indian Express*, 27.5.94, "Attempt to commit *sati* still a punishable offence."
47. *The Indian Express*, 9.5.94, "Psychological trauma is a medical, not legal issue", by L.P. Shah.
48. *The Times of India*, "Never say die", by Bindiya Mathur. 8.5.94.
49. "The Suicide Issue" *The Times of India*, 10.5.94.
50. "*Sati* attempt still punishable" *The Times of India*, 27.5.94.
51. "Tomorrow's Zero-Suicide Society and the Individual, by Jug Suraiya. The *Times of India*, 7.5.94.
52. "Euthanasia—The Thin End of the Wedge", by Eustace J.D. Souza. *The Times of India*, Bombay, 17.5.94.

53. "SC ruling on suicide: where does it leave cops?" *The Indian Express*, 29.6.94.
54. "Unsettling Judgement", *The Indian Express*, 29.4.94.
55. "Suicide bid is no crime, says SC". *The Indian Express*, 28.4.94.
56. *The Indian Express*, 17.5.94, "Suicide is not an act of cowardice", by Avijit Pathak.
57. *The Hindustan Times*, 19.5.94, "Attempted suicide not punishable", by Arvind Kala.
58. *The Hindustan Times*, 9.5.94, "Suicide-Sans deterrent", by Kusum.
59. Archbishop of Delhi and NIC member.
60. "Suicide goes against the Supreme Principle of Life", *The Indian Express*, 9.5.94.
61. "Suicide judgement raises questions", by S.C. Bhattacharya. *The Hindustan Times*, 9.5.94, Letters to the Editors.
62. *Columbia Law Review*, pp. 348–376, vol. LXXXVI - 1986, New York.
63. *The Indian Express*, 7.10.94, "Immolation bid to protest UP shoot out".
64. *The Law Reports*, 1938, p. 586, J.L.
65. *The Times of India*, 7.5.94, "Tomorrow's Zero-Suicide, Society And the Individual", by Jug Suraiya.
66. J.T. 1994(5) SC 528.
67. For critical comments on the point, see also, "Suicide—A Judicial Retreat?", by Kusum. *The Hindustan Times*, 27.9.94.
68. "Should suicide be outside the scope of law? Psychological trauma is a medical not legal issue", by L.P. Shah. *The Indian Express*, 9.5.94.
69. (1990) 3 All ER 246.
70. *Ibid.*
71. *Regina* v. *City of London Coroner, Ex Parte Barbar*, (1975) 1 WLR 1310.
72. *Suffolk University Law Review*, p. 837, vol. XXV, No. 3, Fall, 1991; see also, *News Week*, pp. 38–43, October 17, 1994, "Suicide cult".